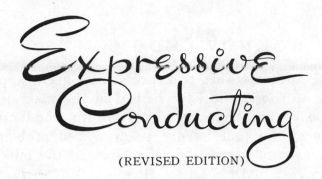

Expressive Conducting

(REVISED EDITION)

Max T. Krone

$2.00

NEIL A. KJOS MUSIC CO., PARK RIDGE, ILL.

ACKNOWLEDGMENTS

The author wishes to express his sincere appreciation to those who have helped in the making of this book: to all the students of his conducting classes of the past twenty years whose problems, questions, and suggestions have formed the bulk of these pages; to Dr. Charles Hirt, and to Dr. Lucien Cailliet, for their careful reading of the manuscript and their many helpful suggestions; and to many other friends who read parts of the manuscript. He is grateful also to Dr. Hirt and to Miss Janice Parker who posed so patiently for the photographs in the chapters on conducting technics, and to Dr. D. Welty Lefever who took the pictures. He is especially indebted to his wife, Beatrice Perham Krone, for her constant helpfulness and suggestions. Many of the ideas expressed in Chapter XI were first worked out by her in music institutes and workshops.

EXPRESSIVE CONDUCTING

CONTENTS

MUSIC EXAMPLES

Expressive Conducting

CHAPTER ONE

THE CONDUCTOR HIMSELF

I love all beauteous things,	*I too will something make*
I seek and adore them;	*And joy in the making;*
God hath no better praise,	*Although tomorrow it seem*
And man in his hasty days	*Like the empty words of a dream*
Is honoured for them.	*Remembered on waking.*

—ROBERT BRIDGES.

It is unfortunately true that a conductor may be a fine musician and be well versed in music literature and technics, and yet, because of a lack of certain personal qualities, may never be successful with choral groups. This is likewise true, although perhaps not to the same extent, with instrumental groups. Singing, however, is so personal an expression, so closely linked to our physical and emotional condition and responses, that personal reactions are especially important in choral groups. Then, too, most singers in choral groups are more concerned with immediate pleasure in performance and less with the development of an individual performing technic than are their instrumental brethren, and any personal traits of a conductor that interfere with or inhibit that pleasurable reaction are likely to bring quick response in the form of a falling off in membership, or halfhearted performance, or both.

Some of these personal qualifications that make for success in the conductor are:

A pleasant, cheerful attitude toward life and his group, coupled with a good sense of humor and plenty of patience. It is not necessary to be saccharine, to wear a "rubber-stamp" smile, or to be a Pollyanna. There are times when the conductor needs to be a taskmaster and a disciplinarian. His performers will admire and like him for it, if they know and feel that he is being severe for the best interests of the group, and that the storm will be followed by the sun.

One of the hardest things for the beginning conductor to learn is patience: patience for endless repetitions; patience with slow thinkers and learners; patience for giving voices and technics time to develop; patience with ears that take time to hear interval and chord relationships; patience when students return to rehearsal unable to sing or play a passage that seemed perfectly learned the day or rehearsal before — always patience.

Tact. Conducting is necessarily a social art. A teacher must ask students, other teachers, and townsfolk to cooperate with and assist him, continually. It is good, common sense to be tactful, considerate and kindly in all relationships with them.

Confidence in his own ability, and the ability to inspire confidence in his group. This is one of those subtle relationships that needs never to be expressed but is easily felt. There is no feeling of vanity on the part of the conductor, but rather a quiet self-assurance that comes from a knowledge of his scores and his ability to teach them to others, of his acquaintanceship with the human voice or with orchestral or band instruments, and his ability to solve the problems that will arise in the learning of the music. He never needs to tell his students that he has this knowledge and ability — they sense its presence or absence quickly enough, and no amount of talking about it will make them believe that the conductor *knows* if he does not.

Sincere love of working with people. No matter how fine a musician he may be, the conductor who dislikes or shies from working with people will never be a success as a choral conductor. Choral singing is probably a social art to a much greater extent than performance in instrumental groups, and the finest choral performance is only possible when there is a fine *esprit de corps* within the group itself, and a friendly, cordial, if not an affectionate relationship between the chorus and the conductor. But with instrumental groups, also, the importance of a friendly and cooperative attitude is most important.

Emotional self-control coupled with the abandon necessary to make music vital. If a conductor cannot control himself, there is little likelihood that he will be able to control others, and certainly he has no place in a schoolroom or church choir loft. We refer here, of course, to flights of temper, frequently called "temperament," in which a conductor sometimes indulges when his own ineffectiveness or lack of experience, or his attempt to accomplish more than his group is capable of, leads to an *impasse* and to temporarily unstrung nerves. The skillful conductor knows the limitations of his group and also knows that if within those limitations the group does not attain the results he expects, the chances are overwhelmingly that the fault lies in his own teaching ability. It is foolish and harmful for the morale of the group in such a case for him to vent his spleen on his performers.

This again is quite another thing from losing himself in the emotional state of the music to the extent that he can let the spirit of it speak through his heart, his face and his eyes to his performers, so that they in turn may let it speak through themselves to their audience. We have acquired inhibitions in our modern life that make it difficult for us to express our emotions without being terribly self-conscious. A singer, however, must also be an actor in the sense that he has a story to tell and a mood to establish. Obviously, it would be foolish for an actor to try to move an audience with a beautiful voice and an expressionless face; it is just as foolish for a singer or a choral conductor to try to do it. An instrumental performer is handicapped somewhat in this matter by having to express himself through an instrument which he holds in his hands and sometimes in his mouth, but even so there is no reason for him to look as if he were bored by his performance.

Imagination. The fine conductor like any other artist must be more than a good craftsman. He must have that precious ability to re-create from the printed page, through his performers, more than appears in those black and white symbols; he must have the ability to hear in his imagination qualities and colors of tone, singly and in combinations; he must feel the surge of a phrase and its coming to rest like a bird settling lightly into its nest; he must envision all the parts of the song in their proper relationship and balance to one another to form a beautifully proportioned work of art.

The ability to impart self-confidence and calm to a group under the stress of public performance. The nervous, excitable conductor places himself and his group under a terrible handicap before a note is performed. The singer's vocal apparatus is so intimately bound up with his body that any physiological changes in the body due to emotions such as fear, or anger, or too intense excitement, or nervousness are reflected immediately in the voice. The instrumentalist's fingers may "freeze" from such excitement. Then, too, under nervous strain, excitement or fear, memory plays strange tricks on us, and many of the fine nuances which were worked out so carefully in rehearsal disappear; or we may even forget notes and words themselves. Calmness and assurance are essential; they must emanate from the conductor to the group.

The desire and ability to learn. The art of music is an endless one. The conductor who becomes satisfied and complacent is lost. First, there must be attained the knowledge and power to secure the proper tone quality and intonation from voices or instruments of all kinds; second, there is the great field of choral and instrumental literature with which to become acquainted; third, there is the actual technic of expressive conducting ever to be improved; fourth, there is the limitless realm of one's own musicianship to be developed; and fifth, there is the opportunity to explore and experiment with the fascinating field of human relationships and psychology. One life is too short for all this. There is no point at which one can say, "Now, I have arrived. There is nothing more for me to learn."

Ability to organize. Some are born with this gift; others acquire it only by dint of sweat and toil; some never achieve it. It is so important because it saves precious time in rehearsals, because a well-organized group takes pride in its smooth functioning, and because it saves so much wear and tear on everyone's nerves, especially the conductor's. Fortunately, it is an ability that usually can be developed.

Ability to let the group learn by singing or playing. One of the most difficult tasks for the young conductor is to keep quiet. As he acquires experience, he *discovers that students learn very little from his talking, and that they learn in inverse proportion to the length of his speeches!* This is always a blow to one's ego, but the wise conductor learns to choose his words well, to demonstrate briefly what he wants, and then to let his performers learn the way we all learn—by our own experience.

A distinct, pleasant speaking voice and a good vocabulary. These are perhaps the least essential of the desirable qualities we have listed, but they are such assets that they should be included. Listening to one's voice is quite easy to do today, with recording equipment so common. Every conductor should make a record of his voice so that he may know what it is his students have to listen to at every rehearsal!

A wonderful adjunct to a pleasant speaking voice is a good vocabulary. It is not necessary to be an orator, but an immediate command of the language, especially of adjectives, is a great asset in getting across to your group your idea of the tone quality, the diction, the rhythm, or the phrasing you want. There is also a danger in having too fluent a vocabulary—it is easy to become too verbose. If you can demonstrate vocally what you want, a good rule to follow is "sing it" when you feel like talking.

Good personal appearance and posture. These are not important solely because it is more pleasant to look at a conductor who is well groomed and has good posture. The latter is especially important for good performance, and the conductor who sets an example of it himself secures a good performing position from his students through unconscious imitation on their part and less nagging on his part.

In conclusion. To what extent a conductor must embody all or part of these qualities, no one can say. Undoubtedly, his chances of success are greater, other things being equal, if he fulfills most of the personal requirements; but "other things" are not always equal. It may be quite possible for a fine musician and teacher to attain real success as a director in spite of decided personal shortcomings, since he may be able to command the respect and admiration of his group because of his musical and conducting ability, and, as Shakespeare sagely observed, "Nothing is good, I see, without respect." But if respect for the conductor's musical and technical ability is accompanied by an equal respect and affection for him as a human being of the type we have described, there is little doubt that he will be a successful conductor. It might be interesting to check yourself with this list occasionally!

CHAPTER TWO

CONDUCTING TWO-BEAT MEASURE

This Backward Man, this View Obstructor
Is known to us as the CONDUCTOR;
He beats the time with grace and vim,
And sometimes they keep up with him.[1]

It is quite possible for a good musician who knows how to handle people, and how to secure good tone and diction from untrained voices, to develop a good chorus without knowing anything of traditional baton technic. Similarly, an instrumental conductor who understands the problems of tone production and fingering of the various instruments, and who has a good ear and good musical judgment, may develop a good orchestra and band even if his conducting is entirely unorthodox. Whether he uses a baton is likewise of minor importance as far as the performance of his groups is concerned.

The quality of the final performance is determined largely in rehearsals where the conductor's job is that of *teacher,* rather than on the concert stage where he appears as *conductor,* and makes certain motions with his hands and arms. These motions may only indicate the tempo, or they may be expressive reminders to the group of certain lessons learned in rehearsal, but at most they are a comparatively minor part of the conductor's musical equipment.

Why learn to conduct in the traditional manner? The answer is similar to the one for the question "Why learn all the sounds that make up our spoken language?" Obviously, it is because both conducting and speech constitute a generally accepted basis for the expression and common understanding of certain ideas. Once learned they save us a tremendous amount of time and effort, and no matter to what group we address ourselves, as long as they too understand our symbols, we are readily understood.

Orchestra and band musicians have come to expect that their conductors will give them the conventional measure patterns or beats because they are helpful in assisting the players to keep their places. Instrumentalists are expected to read music at sight, and their parts are more or less rhythmically independent and often contain long periods of rest. Choralists are not usually confronted

---

[1] From Laurence McKinney—*People of Note.* (New York: E. P. Dutton Co., publishers in the United States.) Used by permission.

by such difficulties and many of them learn their parts largely by rote; consequently, they have not expected or received much in the way of traditional conducting from their directors. For this reason, choral conductors have tended to become careless in their conducting and are usually looked at askance and frequently known as "snake charmers" by instrumental conductors and performers. That such need not be the case is evidenced by the increasing number of young choral conductors who have learned the "conductor's language" and who can conduct either instrumental or choral groups in a musicianly manner.

Posture.   Posture is the first prerequisite in conducting just as it is first in singing.   Stand with the feet about together, and with the weight of the body on the soles of the feet, not on the heels.   Keep the shoulders back and let the arms swing freely. The conductor's posture and attitude should convey confidence and command of the situation. You may have to assume such an attitude in spite of trembling knees at first. Psychologists point out, however, that it is possible to establish an emotional state by first setting up the outward physical expressions of that emotion, so set up an external appearance of confidence and assurance and you will be surprised how quickly these attitudes permeate your whole being.   Then you can give your entire attention to the work at hand.

Conducting patterns.   There are a few conducting patterns that the conductor needs to know, and these should be practiced in front of a mirror, preferably to music—the phonograph and radio provide an easy accompaniment — until they are so automatic that they require no conscious attention.   They are the conductor's "five-finger exercises" and must be performed with the same facility and ease as the pianist does his scales.

Holding the baton.   Whether or not he uses a baton eventually, every conductor should learn *how* to handle it gracefully and easily.   In conducting smaller choral groups, he will probably dispense with it; with larger groups and in conducting a chorus with orchestra or band, he will probably find it easier to secure precision of attack and release, since the end of a baton is a more precise point to follow than a hand.   Then too, it can easily be seen in Fig. 1 that the arc of the beat described by the end of the baton, is many times larger than the arc described by the hand in the same movement and in the same duration of time.   Naturally, it is easier to follow the larger arc.

Conductors vary in the way they hold their batons. The most important thing is that the grip should be firm but not rigid. A light-weight baton, between twelve and fifteen inches long, with a cork grip is easiest to handle and least tiring to use. The suggestions given here for holding the baton have been worked out with many conducting classes and have been found to produce the most satisfactory results in the minimum of time. Adjustments will, of course, have to be made for fingers of different sizes.

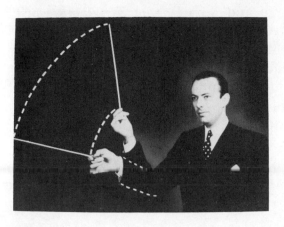

Fig. 1

Hold your right hand[2] out before you with the thumb up. With your left hand place the grip of the baton across your right hand index finger and the second joint of your middle finger. The exact position of the baton across your fingers will depend upon the length of your fingers. Now place your thumb on the baton above your index finger, and curl your first two fingers around the baton. Your other two fingers will naturally curl into place below the end of the baton. See Fig. 1.

Extend your arm and baton horizontally in front of you at the height of your shoulder. Your thumb should be up as in Fig. 2[3]. Do not bend your wrist. Think of the baton as an extension of your hand and forearm, as in Fig. 2. If your baton points straight upward, push upward lightly with your middle finger on the grip of the baton. This will push the *tip* of the baton *down* until the baton is about in a straight line with your forearm. See Figs. 2 and 3.

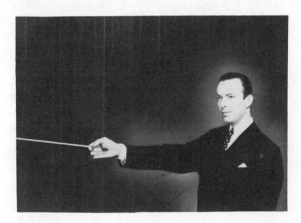

Fig. 2

Fig. 3

[2] Even if you are left-handed. It will be awkward at first, but do not conduct with your left hand; it is confusing to performers and is unnecessary.

[3] It is perfectly all right to hold your hand with the palm down, but it has been our experience with a great many beginning students that there will be fewer mistakes to correct if the hand is held in the way we have suggested at first, and *treated as part of the forearm*. We will use the wrist later, after the use of the forearm has become automatic (see page 43).

Now move your forearm up and down, *from the elbow,* until this motion feels natural. Keep your upper arm stationary, out in front of you, shoulder high, and about parallel to the floor (Fig. 2). Bring the baton back to a vertical position on the up stroke (Fig. 3.). Beginners have a tendency to swing the whole arm from the shoulder. Avoid this. Keep your upper arm out in front of you, about horizontal all the time, until it feels natural to conduct with the forearm only. You need a full-arm stroke comparatively little, only for vigorous, *fortissimo* passages really. Conducting from the elbow will save you a great deal of energy and will look much better. We will use the whole arm later.

Conducting two-beat measure. You have just been conducting two beats to the measure. The down beat is "one" (the first beat in any meter is down). The up beat is "two" (the last beat of the measure in any meter is up). The type of beat you have been making is rather angular, however. This is easily overcome by allowing the down beat to curve a little to the right at the end of the stroke, and then letting it retrace its path on the way up.

As the baton comes down, let your forearm turn slightly (Fig. 5C) so that at the bottom of the stroke your palm is down (Fig. 5D). *Do not move your hand from the wrist.* Keep it a part of the forearm at this stage of your development. In Fig. 5 follow the position of the hand at various stages of the down beat. Notice the *preparatory* or *cue* beat, which serves to get the group ready for the attack on the first beat of the composition. More will be said of the preparatory beat later.

Do not let your baton fall below the level of vision of your group. *The first beat occurs at the bottom of the stroke* (at the arrowhead in Fig. 4 or at the horizontal line of Fig. 5D), and if the performers cannot see the baton at that point they can hardly be expected to know the exact moment of the beat. The dotted line to the right of this point in the two figures represents the rebound, which prepares the baton for the second beat.

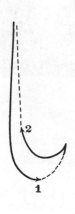

On the up stroke, retrace the path of the baton as indicated in Fig. 4. The second beat occurs at the point at which your hand changes to a vertical motion, as indicated by the arrowhead in Fig. 4. The dotted line above this point represents the rebound which prepares for the next down beat.

Fig. 4

Turn your forearm so that your hand is vertical most of the way up (thumb up). Feel the beat at the *tip* of the baton, not at your hand. Keep your upper arm parallel to the floor all the while. *Do not swing your arm from the shoulder.* Imagine that each beat is painting the design of an inverted cane in the air as in Fig. 4.

It may help to give your beat decision and clarity if you make a very slight pause at each of the arrowheads of Fig. 4, as if you were dividing each beat into two parts.

Conduct the excerpt from *Morning Song*[4], page 10, with a strong, *marcato* beat, using only your forearm. Conduct *Autumn Song*[5], page 11, with a more flowing, *legato* beat. *Per Spelmann*[5], page 12, is written in a *compound* meter[6], and would be conducted two beats to the measure also, since the tempo is moderately fast. A dotted quarter note gets a beat.

Fig. 5. **The Down Beat.**

NOTE: The photographs on this page were reversed in printing so that the motions would coincide in direction with those you make with your *right* hand *as you look at the pictures.* Imagine that you are looking at yourself in a mirror.

A. Start of Preparatory Stroke.

C. Midway Down.
Note that the hand is beginning to turn.

B. End of Preparatory Stroke;
Beginning of Down Stroke.

D. End of Down Stroke.
Note that the palm is down.

---

[4] From *Songs to Sing With Descants*—Beatrice Perham Krone (Kjos).
[5] From *Songs of Sweden and Finland*—B. Krone and R. Ostlund (Kjos).

[6] See page 27.

Morning Song [7]

(Excerpt)

B.P.K.

Allegro

Czech Folk Melody
Arr. by Beatrice Perham Krone

PIANO

O - ver the mead-ows at break of day, Na - ture is call - ing as

if to say, "Come out, my com - rades, Come out, my com - rades,

All the world's joy - ful this A - pril day!" day!"

[7]From Songs To Sing With Descants —Krone (Kjos)

Autumn Song [8]
(Round)

Text by R.O. and M.T.K.

Finnish Folk Song
Arr. by B.P.K.

1. Here I sit and wait for you,
2. Fall is in the air to-day,

'Neath the spread-ing branch-es, Cool the grass with shade and dew, Sun-light 'round me
Hear the wild geese cry - ing, Come out-doors with-out de - lay, Snow will soon be

Refrain

danc - es. Hei, lu, li - a, li - a - la, Loud my voice is ring - ing.
fly - ing. Hei, lu, li - a, li - a - la, Come and join my sing - ing.

* The second voice enters when the first voice reaches here.
[8] From Songs of Sweden and Finland – Krone and Ostlund (Kjos)

Per Spelmann [9]

(Peter, the Player)

Conducting a fast 6/8 is no different than conducting a 2/4 measure, except that in 6/8 there is a "background" feeling of three equal divisions of each beat, while in 2/4 there is a "background" feeling of two divisions of the beat. Make a decided and noticeable division of each beat in the *ritardando* at the end of the song. A dotted quarter note, not an eighth note, is the beat note. See Chapter IX, page 55.

Text adapted from translation by
B. P. K.

Scandinavian Folk Song
Arr. by B.P.K.

* Per has a little trouble tuning his fiddle here.

CHAPTER THREE

CONDUCTING FOUR-BEAT MEASURE

Music is the essence of harmony existing between heaven, earth and man.

—ANCIENT CHINESE.

NOTE: The pictures on this page were reversed in printing so that the motions would coincide in direction with those you make with your *right* hand *as you look at the pictures.* Imagine that you are looking at yourself in a mirror.

Fig. 6. **Four-Beat Measure.**

A. The End of the Preparatory Stroke. Beginning of the Down Stroke.

B. End of the Down Stroke.

The first beat of a four-beat measure is just like that of a two-beat measure. Instead of beating upward for "two", however, move your hand horizontally across your body, to the left, palm down, simply by bending your elbow, *not* by swinging your arm from the shoulder. See Fig. 6C.

On the third beat, move your hand to the right across your body, by straightening your arm horizontally *from the elbow.* At the end of the stroke, your arm should be almost straight, your palm down, and your baton should be extended as a continuation of your forearm. See Fig. 6D.

On the fourth beat, bring your hand in towards your right ear, as in Fig. 6E. Do not move your upper arm, just swing your forearm from the elbow. Your hand gradually turns from a horizontal position (palm down) to a vertical position (thumb up) as

C. End of Second Stroke.

D. End of Third Stroke.

E. End of Up Stroke.

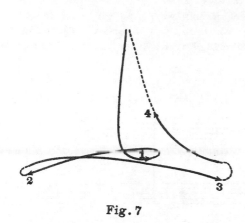

Fig. 7

your baton moves upward. Notice that you trace the pattern of the inverted cane on this beat, just as in the up beat of two-beat measure, except that here the "cane" is tilted a little. The complete pattern for the four beats is outlined in Fig. 7.

Note: the first beat occurs at the *bottom* of the down stroke (at the arrowhead of Fig. 7), and lasts until the farthest point to the left of the second stroke where the second beat occurs. The third beat occurs at the farthest point to the right of the third stroke, and lasts until the arrowhead of the up stroke, where the fourth beat occurs.

Whether or not your side strokes curve as in Fig. 7, or as in Fig. 6C and D, is immaterial. Some conductors prefer one way and some the other. Some simply conduct all horizontal strokes as straight lines. Many like to end each side stroke with a downward dip of the baton as is indicated in Fig. 7.

Conduct *These Things Shall Be*[1], page 16, first with four beats to the measure, and then as *alla breve*, ¢ , a broad two-beat measure. Practice changing from 4/4 to 2/2 until you can do it easily and gracefully.

Now read pages 39 to 41, and then practice the two chorales on pages 18 and 42. Feel each beat in these two songs as a divided beat consisting of two equal divisions. This serves two purposes: it gives a rhythmic surge to the song that keeps it alive and vital, and it prevents you from setting too fast a tempo. These are majestic hymns and there should be a breadth and dignity in their performance which is lost if they are sung too fast.

In *Now Thank We All Our God*[1], the meter changes from 4/4 to 4/2 but the *beat* remains constant in duration. That means that a quarter note in 4/2 will receive the same amount of time as an eighth note in 4/4.

Read the notes on "Changes in Meter", pages 59 and 60, and then practice the songs on pages 62 to 66. We recommend that you study the chapters on *Rhythmic Relationships,* Chapters IX and X, along with the next few chapters of the text.

---

[1] From *Great Songs of Faith*—The Krones (Kjos)

These Things Shall Be [2]

We can think of no better hymn for "a world in tune" than this one. John Symonds, the English poet, has caught the spirit of the brotherhood of man with a poet's vision in words of beauty and strength, to match a great tune composed a hundred years earlier. The hymn with his words was not used extensively however until World War I. Later it appeared in the League of Nations Song Book.

John A. Symonds, 1880

from Psalmodia Evangelica, 1789
Arr. by the Krones, Beatrice and Max

1. These things shall be, a loft-ier race Than e'er the world hath
3. Na - tion with na - tion, land with land, Un - armed shall live as

known shall rise, With flame of free - dom in ___ their ___ souls, And
com - rades free; In ev - 'ry heart and brain ___ shall ___ throb The

light of knowl - edge in their eyes.
pulse of one ___ fra - ter - ni - ty.

(After 3rd stanza only) These things shall be!

[2]From Great Songs of Faith — Krone (Kjos)

Now Thank We All Our God[3]

(THANKSGIVING CHORALE)

Johann Crüger was one of the greatest hymn writers of the Lutheran Church. This one, as well as *Jesu, Priceless Treasure*, and *Bedeck Thyself, O My Soul*, have been loved and sung by countless thousands for the past three hundred years.

Martin Rinkart (1586-1649)
Eng. translation by Catherine Winkworth

Johann Crüger (1598-1662)
Arr. by the Krones, Beatrice and Max

★ NOTE: Sing the first stanza in unison, the second as a duet.

[3]From Great Songs of Faith — Krone (Kjos)

Copyright 1944 by Max and Beatrice Krone
Published by Neil A. Kjos Music Co., Chicago

from our moth - ers' arms Hath blessed us on our way With
keep us_ in His grace, And guide_ us when per - plexed, And

count - less gifts of love, And_ still_ is_ ours to - day.
free us from all ills In_ this_ world and the next.

Broadly (♩ = ♩, app.)

DESCANT

3. All praise and thanks be to God, the Fa-ther, The Fa - ther, now be_ giv - en,

MELODY

3. All praise and thanks to God, The Fa - ther, now be - giv - en, The

8va

CHAPTER FOUR

CONDUCTING THREE-BEAT MEASURE

. . . Music . . . is like a voice,
A low voice calling fancy, or a friend
To the green woods in the gay summer time.

—ROBERT BROWNING.

NOTE: The pictures on this page were reversed in printing so that the motions would coincide in direction with those you make with your *right* hand *as you look at the the pictures.* Imagine that you are looking at yourself in a mirror.

Fig. 8. **Three-Beat Measure.**

A. End of Preparatory Beat.
Beginning of Down Stroke.

The first beat in three-beat measure is down, but with the rebound to the left instead of the right. Think of the inverted cane again, but with the curved handle turned to your left. As your hand descends, let your forearm turn so that for most of the stroke your palm is down, just as it has been before, but let your hand move to a point *in front of* your body so that you will be in position to beat to the right for the second beat of the measure

B. End of Down Stroke.

C. End of Second Stroke.

D. End of Third Stroke.

(see Fig. 8B). For the second beat move your hand across your body to the right *by straightening your arm from the elbow* just as in the case of the third beat of four-beat measure (see Fig. 8C). The last beat of the measure is up, and in towards your

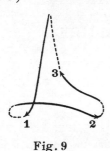

Fig. 9

right ear just like the last beat of four-beat measure (see Fig. 8D). The complete diagram for three-beat measure is given in Fig. 9.

Practice the excerpts from *A Thanksgiving Hymn*[1], page 23, and *We Wish You a Merry Christmas*[1], page 26. Since both songs begin on the third beat of the measure, give a preparatory or cue beat to your *right* and bring the chorus in on the third (up) beat. Now try Brahms' *Lullaby*[2], page 24.

Three-in-One

At faster tempos, three-beat measure is conducted with only one beat to the measure. Practice this by starting slowly with three beats; then gradually accelerate the tempo, making the second beat smaller and smaller until it becomes simply a slight pause at the end of the down-beat. To return to three beats to the measure, gradually slow up the tempo and increase the size of the second beat until you are conducting three beats to the measure again. *We Wish You a Merry Christmas* is good for this practice.

[1] From *Songs to Sing with Descants* (Kjos).
[2] From *From Descants to Trios*—The Krones (Kjos).

A Thanksgiving Hymn [3]
(Excerpt)

B. P. K.

Melody from Geistliche Kirchengesänge (1623)
Arr. by Beatrice Perham Krone

Maestoso

1. To God on high our songs we raise, To him we sing our thank-ful praise, Al - le - lu - ia, Al - le - lu - ia. With grate - ful heart and glad - some voice, Let all who love the Lord re - joice, Al - le - lu - ia, Al - le - lu - ia, Al - le - lu - ia, Al - le - lu - ia, Al - le - lu - ia.

[3] From Songs to Sing With Descants — Krone (KJos)

Lullaby [4]

JOHANNES BRAHMS
Arr. by B. and M. K.

* If autoharp is used, strum the accompaniment in the rhythm of the piano part for both stanzas.

4 From *From Descants to Trios* — Krone (Kjos)

We Wish You a Merry Christmas [5]

(Excerpt)

Traditional English Folk Song
Arr. by Beatrice Perham Krone

PIANO

1. We wish you a Mer-ry Christ-mas, We wish you a Mer-ry Christ-mas, We wish you a Me-ry Christ-mas, And a Hap-py New Year!

[5] From Songs to Sing With Descants — Krone (Kjos)

CHAPTER FIVE

CONDUCTING COMPOUND METERS

Great music is a physical storm agitating to fathomless depths the mystery of the past within us.

—PAUL ELMER MORE.

Conducting Six-beat Measure

Six-beat measure, such as 6/8 or 6/4, is really two-beat measure with each beat divided into three parts. It is therefore said to be a *compound* meter.[1] Frequently, however, in slower tempos or in *rallentandi,* it is necessary to beat six beats. There are several different patterns for six beats to the measure which are used by different conductors. Two of them are suggested here. The first one, illustrated in Fig. 10, is basically a two-beat measure with each beat divided into three parts. It permits an easy transition to a straight two-beat measure, and it gives a change of direction to the baton on the secondary accent (the fourth beat) of the measure, which is important. Many conductors prefer the diagram of Fig. 11, however. It is easy to remember since there is one down beat, two beats to the left, two to the right, and one up. Some conductors conduct it down-left-left-right-up-up, also.

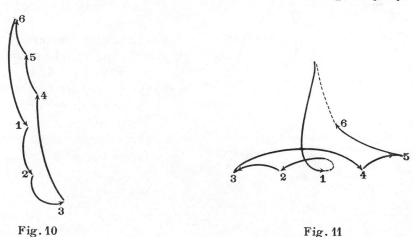

Fig. 10   Fig. 11

The *Christmas Song*[2], page 29, is good practice for 6/8. So, also, are *Silent Night, Sweet and Low* and *Drink to Me Only with Thine Eyes.* Practice changing from six beats to a slow, flowing two-beat measure, and back to six beats again, until this process becomes automatic.

---

[1] See Chapter IX, page 55.
[2] From *Songs of Norway and Denmark*—Krone and Ostlund (Kjos).

Conducting Nine-beat Measure

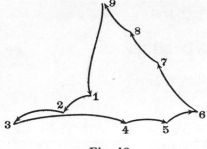

Fig. 12

Nine-beat measure is really a three-beat measure with each beat divided into three parts, so it is also a compound meter.[3] The main outline of beats therefore, is that of a three-beat measure.

The Gaelic Folksong, *Glory to God*, page 31, is good for practice of .nine-beat measure.

Conducting Twelve-beat Measure

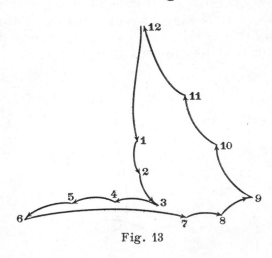

Fig. 13

Twelve - beat measure should be thought of as four-beat measure with each beat divided into three parts. It is also a compound meter.[4] The principal and secondary accents (1, 4, 7, 10), therefore, are indicated in the same directions as the beats of four-beat measure. Practice the excerpt from the *Pastoral Symphony* from *The Messiah,* page 34.

---

[3] See page 55.
[4] See page 55.

Drink To Me Only With Thine Eyes

BEN JOHNSON

OLD ENGLISH
Arr. by The Krones

30

GLORY TO GOD [4]
(Christmas)

B.P.K.

OLD GAELIC FOLK TUNE
Text and arr. by the Krones, Beatrice and Max.

1. Once long a - go in Beth - le - hem's man - ger, Je - sus was born in ox - en stall, Proph - ets fore - told Him, wise - men a -
2. Je - sus our Sav - ior, Lord and Re - deem - er, Here in our hearts will ev - er be - long, Teach us a - gain to love one an -

[4]From Our Third Book of Descants — Krone (Kjos)

32

dored Him, An-gels pro-claimed Him, Lord of all.
oth-er, As we a-dore Thee now in song.

dored Him, An-gels pro-claimed Him, Lord of all.
oth-er, As we a-dore Thee now in song.

mf *cresc.*

Broadly
★ HIGHS
mf

3. Let the world sing, _____ "Glo-ry and hon-or, Glo-ry to God!

MIDDLES
Melody
mf

3. Let the world sing, _____ "Glo-ry and hon-or, to Him who

LOWS *mp* *f*

3. Let the world sing, "Glo-ry and hon-or, to Him who

mf **Broadly**

★ The High part may be played by a violin and the voices divided between the Middle and Low parts if desired.

Excerpt from the
Pastoral Symphony
From the Messiah

G. F. HANDEL

CHAPTER SIX

CUE BEATS: DIVIDED BEATS: THE FERMATA

Servant and Master am I:
Servant of those dead, master of those living,
Through my spirit immortals speak the message
that makes the world weep and laugh, and wonder and worship . . .
For I am the instrument of God. I am MUSIC.

—Anonymous.

The Cue, Preparatory, or "Breath" Beat.

Purposes. The cue beat serves two important purposes:

1. It gives the performers warning to get ready, and a signal to breathe before they start singing or playing.

2. It establishes the tempo.

Amateur singers and wind instrument players always wait until time to begin singing or playing before they breathe, and then, since it is impossible to do both at once, they fail to attack cleanly. Be sure that you have the eyes of your group on your baton before you start, and then if the cue beat is not enough of a reminder to breathe, breathe with them, through your mouth, as you give the cue beat.

Just as it requires only two points to establish a straight line, so it usually requires only two beats to establish a tempo, the cue beat and the first beat of the composition. It is not necessary to give more than one preparatory beat *if* you have thoroughly set the tempo *within yourself* before you start conducting. *This is important.* Never start until you have sung a phrase to yourself first at the tempo you wish it to go.

Direction. The cue beat is ordinarily in the direction of the beat just preceding the first beat of the piece. Thus, in 4/4 meter, if the music starts on "one", give an up beat (four) for the cue; if it starts on *four,* give *three* as the cue, and so on. It is well to count *to yourself* all the beats of the measure which contains the cue beat, making the preparatory beat *in tempo* as you come to it. Thus, in 4/4, if the piece begins on *four,* count to yourself, "one, two-," then as you think "three", make the cue beat to the right, and then bring in the chorus or orchestra on *four.*

Cue on "half-past". If the piece begins on the last half of a beat, the problem is a little more complicated. A good general rule to follow in this case is to figure out in which direction you should beat the first note of the song, then give the cue beat in some direction at an angle to this direction so that your hand will be in position to begin the beat for the first note.

For example, practice starting *Carmencita,* page 64. The first note must be conducted with an up stroke, and a cue beat either to the right or left will place the hand in position for this beat. Remember, the cue beat must be only half a beat in duration. It would be logical to give the cue beat in the direction of *four* (up), but then the cue beat and the beat for the beginning note both would be up, and it would be difficult for the chorus to see when one stroke ends and the other begins. Until you have had considerable experience, it is safer to count to yourself all the beats in the measure containing the cue beat, *in tempo,* dividing each beat, thus, *"one-ta two-ta three-ta-",* conducting the cue beat in tempo on *four,* and bringing in the chorus on *ta.*

Cue on last fourth of the beat. If the music begins on a note a fourth of a beat long, as in *The Sailor,*[1] page 37, the cue should consume three-fourths of the beat. In the case of *The Sailor* the cue beat may be down, or preferably, sideways, since the beat of the first note itself is down.

Cue on a third of the beat. If the song begins on the second third of the beat, as in the excerpt from *'Tis Irish I Am,*[2] page 38, let the cue beat consume one-third of the beat. If it begins on the last third of the beat as would be the case if the same song began after the introduction, let the cue beat consume two-thirds of the beat. Conduct the cue beat at right angles to the beat of the first note, as before.

Remember:
1. Make the cue beat *in tempo.* Sing a phrase or count a measure to yourself before you start.

2. Do not make the cue beat too large or vigorous, for if you do, someone will start on it instead of on the first note.

3. Don't start the group with your eyes in the score, or with that abstracted, far-away look that beginning conductors are likely to have in their eyes. Have direct glance contact with every performer before you give the cue beat.

4. Be sure the cue beat is in a different direction from the first beat of the piece, and that it will bring your hand into the right position for the first note.

[1] From *Spanish and Latin American Songs*—Beatrice and Max Krone (Kjos).
[2] Published in octavo form by the Kjos Music Co.

THE SAILOR (Excerpt)
(El Marinero)
S.A.T.B. or Two Equal Voices

CHILEAN SAILOR SONG

PIANO

Sturdily

TENOR (Soprano) and BASS (Alto)

1. The boat of the stur-dy sail-or__ Fears__ no storm at
2. The sail-or who braves the o-cean, Rid-ing the rag-ing
La bar-ca del ma-ri-ne-ro__ ya__ no te-me el

sea, no storm at sea; No mat-ter the wind or weath-er,__
foam, the rag-ing foam; Will know when the dan-ger's o-ver,__
mar, no te-me el mar. Si a-ca-so ha-ya un vien-to__

Sail-or and boat are free, they both are free.
And be re-turn-ing home, re-turn-ing home.
vie-ne la tem-pes-tad, la tem-pes-tad.

Sail-or and boat are free, they both are free.
And be re-turn-ing home, re-turn-ing home.
vie-ne la tem-pes-tad, la tem-pes-tad.

[3] From Spanish and Latin American Songs — Krone (Kjos)

'Tis Irish I Am (Excerpt) [4]

Two-part Boys, Girls or Mixed Voices

M.T.K.

Arranged from four Irish tunes *
By the KRONES, BEATRICE and MAX

Lyrics:

1. 'Tis Irish I am, and 'tis proud I am of it; Though far I wander, Killarney's me home. I'll love her green meadows, her lakes and her colleens, And wear her shamrock wherever I roam.

*In order of their appearance: Irish Washerwoman, Father O'Flynn, Molly on the Shore and Larry O'Gaff.

¹Published separately by Kjos Music Co. Ed. No. 4205

Divided Beats

Two-beat measure.

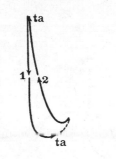

Fig. 14

Three-beat measure.

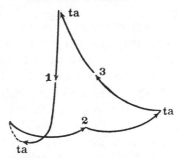

Fig. 15

In slow tempos or in a *ritardando,* it is frequently necessary to indicate the division of the beats with the baton.[5]   The only thing the conductor needs to remember in such cases is to conduct each of the beats in the same general direction as the first part of the beat.   Thus, two-, three-, and four-beat measures with each beat divided into two equal parts would be conducted as indicated in Figs. 14, 15 and 16.

Six-, nine-, and twelve-beat measures are really two-, three-, and four-beat meters with each beat divided into *three* parts.   See the diagrams for these measures on pages 27 and 28.

Four-beat measure.

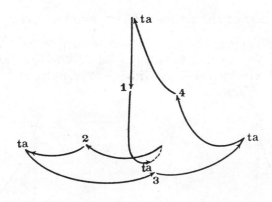

Fig. 16

The Fermata, Pause, or Hold (⌒)

There are two things to observe about *fermatas*:

1. **Getting into the pause.** If the *fermata* occurs on a note which is one beat or less in value and which occurs on the last beat of the measure, simply hold your hand out in front of you at the level of your eyes, at the end of the up stroke, as long as you

---

5 *Chorales* are commonly conducted in this way. See pages 41 and 42.

wish to make the pause. If the *fermata* occurs on any other than the last beat of the measure, change the direction of the beat so that the stroke ends with the baton up in front of you. For instance, in 4/4 meter:

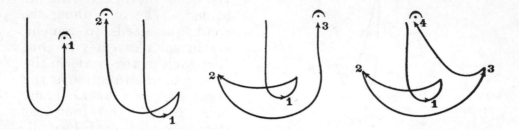

A. Fermata on *one*.   B. Fermata on *two*   C. Fermata on *three*.   D. Fermata on *four*.

Fig . 17

If the *fermata* occurs over a note longer in value than one beat, the safest thing for the beginning conductor to do is to beat out the value of the note, using small beats, and then bring the baton up in front of him with his hand at the level of his eyes, on the last beat of the note. The reason for this is that the inexperienced conductor will usually fail to hold a long note for its full value if he stops beating on the first beat of the note. As the conducting movements become automatic, the pause may be made on the first beat of the note while you count out to yourself the appropriate number of beats for it. It is well to make some slight motion of the baton during the hold to remind your performers to keep sustaining the tone.

   2.   **Getting out of the pause.** There are two ways of doing this:

      a. By releasing the note and making a break in the music while the performers breathe. This is done by making a fast, downward, slashing movement either to the right or left, thus:

A.   Release to the left.   **Fig . 18**   B.   Release to the right.

      The same slashing beat is used at the end of a piece for the final release.

      b. By having the performers "sneak" breath as they sustain the note, and then continuing without the entire group making a break in the flow of tone at the same time.

Continuing after the hold is indicated by making a little preparatory dip with the end of the baton when you are ready to continue, in order to bring the baton into position to make the stroke which the next note requires. See Fig. 19.

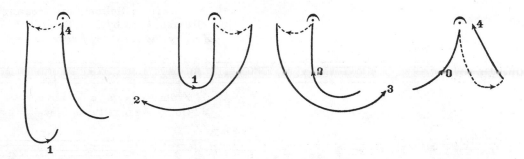

A. Continuing on *one*.   B. Continuing on *two*.   C. Continuing on *three*.   D. Continuing on *four*.

Fig. 19

The fermata in chorales.   There is a difference of opinion among musicians as to how long to hold the ends of phrases in chorales.   We suggest that you think of these songs as what they actually are, congregational hymns, and make the pause in keeping with the musical and textual structure. [6]   Thus, a hold in the *middle* of a musical or textual sentence would be quite short, perhaps non-existent, while a *fermata* at the *close* of a musical or textual sentence, or at the end of a section, would be longer, usually two or three beats longer than normal.

These chorales provide excellent material for practice in getting into and out of *fermatas*.   In the case of phrases where the music or words suggest that the singers continue without a break, leave the *fermata* as suggested in Fig. 19.   Where the phrase definitely ends, make a release as in Fig. 18.

---

[6] For a further discussion of the *chorale* see Max T. Krone, *The Chorus and Its Conductor*, Chap. VIII, Kjos Music Co.

From Heaven Above [7]
(CHORALE)

We have come to associate the name of Bach with the word *chorale* so much that we are likely to forget that he wrote comparatively few *chorale* melodies himself, preferring to take the great hymn tunes of the Lutheran Church of his day and to harmonize them beautifully and often in many different ways.   This is one of the great Christmas hymns of all time.★

Martin Luther

from Schumann's Gesangbuch
Harmonized by J. S. Bach (1685-1750)
Arr. by the Krones, Beatrice and Max

★ One of his more elaborate settings of this same *chorale*, for mixed voices, is published by the publisher of this work, in octavo form, No. 506.

[7]From Great Songs of Faith — Krone (Kjos)

CHAPTER SEVEN

EXPRESSIVE CONDUCTING: RECITATIVE

The man that hath no music in himself,
Nor is not moved with concord of sweet sounds,
Is fit for treasons, stratagems and spoils;
The motions of his spirit are dull as night,
And his affections dark as Erebus;
Let no such man be trusted.

—Shakespeare.

Making the Beats Fit the Character of the Music

So far we have said nothing about the *size* and *character* of the beats in relationship to the music being conducted. It has been our experience that the beginning conductor will have no difficulty here if he takes plenty of time to establish a smooth, flowing, graceful beat using *only* the forearm, bending his arm at the elbow, keeping his upper arm horizontal and practically stationary, with no swing of the arm from the shoulder. Once this beat feels natural and comfortable, other types of beats are easily mastered.

The hinges. There are three "hinges" which the conductor needs to use in expressive conducting:

1. **The elbow hinge** is the one you have been using, and is the best all-purpose hinge. It brings the forearm and hand only into play.

2. **The shoulder hinge** is used only when a *fortissimo* or vigorous effect demands the use of the whole arm. It is often necessary to use the whole arm to build climaxes with large choruses, but it is rarely used with a small group since such sweeping strokes would be out of place.

3. **The wrist hinge** is used when smaller beats are called for by the music—in quieter passages. You should be able to move your hand in either of two ways when conducting from the wrist:

   a. Up and down, with palm down. In this position do not let your hand droop from your wrist. At the bottom of the stroke your hand should be in line with your forearm, not lower than the arm. For the upstroke, raise your hand until it is at a forty-five degree angle to your forearm.

b.   Sideways, with palm down. At the end of the stroke to the right, the long lower joint of your thumb, which connects to the wrist, should be in a straight line with your forearm. Do not carry your hand farther to the right. At the end of the left stroke, the lower joint of your thumb should be at a forty-five degree angle to your forearm.

The same stroke may be used for up and down beats by turning the hand over, to a vertical position.

Size and speed of the beat. The proper size and vigor of each beat depends upon its place in the measure and phrase, and upon the general level of dynamics of the particular passage. The principal and secondary accents of the measure and phrase should receive more stress and longer beats than unaccented beats, of course. The choice of hand, forearm or whole-arm beats depends upon the relative dynamic power of the passage. In any event do not beat rigidly, with each beat as long and as strong as every other one. Your musical training and judgment must decide just how important each beat must be.

Not only should the size and vigor of the beat be appropriate to its place in the phrase and measure, the speed of the beat from its start to its end also should be in keeping with the tempo and character of the music. This may seem obvious, but the beginning conductor often has a tendency to make all beats at the same speed, pausing at the end of the stroke in slower tempi to wait for the next beat to begin. Naturally, such a beat is disturbing to follow. Try to adjust your stroke to the tempo and character of the music so that in slower, *legato* passages the stroke fills the time between beats. In *staccato* passages, and in rapid tempi your baton will have to move quickly from one beat to the next, pausing at one beat until the last possible moment before moving on to the next.

Character of the beat. It is no more unmusical to "beat loud" when the music is soft, than to use the same *kind* of beat for all types of music. A lullaby, a patriotic marching song, and a delicate, tripping song of elves or fairies, each requires a different type of beat. The first calls for a flowing, graceful, restrained *legato;* the second, a vigorous, more angular *marcato;* and the third, a light, weightless *staccato* from the wrist. But also there must be a difference in bodily attitude and facial expression for each type of song, otherwise, the effect is like that produced by an amateur actor who looks in one direction and points in another.

Cueing Parts

In most choral music it is perfectly possible to do everything with the right hand alone, plus appropriate facial expressions— to indicate the beats in the measure, the relative importance of the beats, the general level of dynamics at any given time, the character of the song or passage, and even the cueing of parts.

As a general rule, it is well to indicate the entrance of any part that has a rest of over two measures. This may be done with the right hand without disturbing the measure pattern simply by looking at the entering section, and by making the beat on which they enter end in their direction. If the entering section is on the right side of the conductor and they enter on a left stroke, the conductor can turn the plane of his body to the right so that when the left stroke ends the baton will be pointing directly at the entering section. Similar changes in the plane of the body or of the beats themselves make it possible to bring in any section on any beat.

Practice the excerpt from *The Keeper*,[1] page 50, imagining first that the descant (upper staff) singers are to your right, then again with them on your left.

The left hand. If so much can be done with the right hand and facial expressions, what is the contribution of the left hand? It has several uses:

1. To emphasize a *pianissimo, fortissimo, crescendo, decrescendo* or *rallentando*. To indicate a *pianissimo,* hold your left hand in front of you, close to your chest. A sudden *pianissimo* may be indicated by bringing the hand quickly from out in front of you, back to your chest. For a *decrescendo,* start with your hand up in front of you, palm down, and gradually bring it down and in towards your chest. Conduct small beats with your right hand, of course.

    For a *fortissimo* extend your arm upwards at about a forty-five degree angle, with the palm of your hand up. Imagine you are holding an iron ball in your hand. Tense your muscles. For a *crescendo,* gradually lift your hand, imagining that the iron ball is in it. In sweeping *fortissimo* passages or in a broad *ritardando,* the left hand may duplicate the motions of the right hand to build up a climax or to emphasize the retardation, but *as a general rule, the left hand should not be used merely to duplicate the right hand movements*. Its purpose is to reinforce the right hand when changes or extremes of dynamics or tempo are called for.

    For a sudden contrast from *forte* to *piano* (*fp*), either bring your hands back to your chest very quickly and continue beating small beats, or if you want to be more dramatic, stop beating for an instant. The latter will probably get more attention than just drawing your hands in towards your body.

2. Although it is possible to indicate entering parts with the right hand, as we have pointed out, it is often easier, simpler, and clearer just to point to the entering section with the left hand.

3. To indicate a *fermata* or sustained tone in one or more of the parts while the other parts continue to move. For example,

---

[1] From *Our First Songs to Sing With Descants* (Kjos).

in *Now Thank We All*, page 18, at the end of each phrase in the third stanza, the left hand may indicate the long notes of the melody while the right hand continues to beat for the descant. The left hand indicates the swell for the voices. This would be done by combining the motions for the *crescendo* and *decrescendo* described in (1) above.

4. Sometimes in conducting a large chorus, band or orchestra, or chorus with orchestra, when the performers are spread over a wide area, it is necessary to duplicate the beats of the right hand with the left in order that everyone may see the beat.

In order to develop independence of the two hands, practice making a circle in the air with your left hand, in a counter-clockwise direction while you conduct each of the common meters with your right hand. Make one circle for each beat. Practice also making a *crescendo* and *diminuendo* with your left hand while you conduct the beats with your right, as indicated in the excerpt from *Carmencita*,[2] page 64.

Conducting Recitative

Sooner or later every choral conductor will want to conduct a cantata or oratorio involving soloists, chorus, and orchestra. The most disturbing new factor here is the *recitative,* which carries the story forward in prose, *parlando.* Since a soloist is given a certain amount of freedom in singing recitative, the custom is for the conductor to indicate the beginning of each measure only, with a downbeat, unless the orchestral accompaniment involves more than one note to the measure, in which case it is desirable to indicate the other beats of the measure also. But, even here, the conductor follows the soloist, usually, and adjusts the speed of his beats to the changes in time values made by the soloist. *It is especially important that the orchestra be given a clear down-beat every time a measure bar is passed,* since most of the players will have rests to count out. They should also be given a preparatory beat before the down beat of each measure so that the performers may be ready for the first beat of the measure.

If the soloist is accompanied only by a keyboard instrument, the conductor does not usually conduct at all; the accompanist follows the soloist.

You will notice in the excerpts from the recitatives preceding the *Glory to God* chorus from *The Messiah*,[3] pages 48 and 49, that certain traditional changes are indicated. The following general practices are usually carried out in performances of eighteenth century recitative:

---

2 From *Songs to Sing With Descants* (Kjos).
3 From *Eight Festival Choruses from The Messiah*—Handel-Krone (Kjos)

1. The dominant and tonic chords concluding a section are usually played *after* the soloist has finished, even though they are written to coincide with his last note or two. See page 49. There are occasional exceptions to this when the end of the recitative leads rhythmically into the following aria or chorus.

2. When a phrase ends with two notes on the same pitch, the first one is usually replaced either with a *passing note* (page 49, measure 1), an *appoggiatura* (page 48, measure 1), or a *repetition of the note preceding the last two notes* (page 48, *And Lo!*, measure 3).

    Some conductors, however, would not substitute an *appoggiatura* for the written note in the case of an ascending stepwise passage such as that in the first measure of *And the Angel Said,* page 49.

It is always best to study the recitatives of an important choral work with someone who is an authority in the field before you conduct it.

In conclusion. We have said so much about the technics of conducting that it might be well for us to emphasize again that these are simply your "five-finger exercises," to be mastered as quickly as possible so that all of your attention may be devoted to your principal function as a *conductor,* i.e., providing a means by which something of beauty *flows* from the composer's score *through* your group *to* your audience.

In rehearsals, you must be more a teacher than a conductor—there you and your students labor together to make the message of the music yours. At the concert, however, you have your real opportunity of inspiring your performers with your zeal and enthusiasm for the music they are performing. Your conducting technic must be so thoroughly mastered that it does not inhibit that enthusiasm but instead helps you to make it intelligible, convincing, and moving.

---

4 See Max T. Krone, *The Chorus and Its Conductor,* Kjos Music Co., Chap. III—*The Rehearsal,* Chap. VII—*Interpretation,* and Chap. IX—*The Concert.*

GLORY TO GOD [5]

INTRODUCTORY RECITATIVES

From The Messiah

GEORGE F. HANDEL
(1685-1759)
Edited by Max T. Krone

The recitatives have been included in this edition since they form the proper introduction to the chorus, and since it is quite feasible to do them with several unison sopranos when no one solo voice is available. In the case of high school festival choruses, also, it is often desirable to give many students the opportunity to sing the solos, and an edition is necessary which gives the customary changes in notation if all the soloists are to be prepared in the same manner. Händel indicated few dynamic markings. These have been placed in brackets. The added ones are the Editor's.

THERE WERE SHEPHERDS ABIDING IN THE FIELD (No. 14)

Luke ii: 8

AND LO! THE ANGEL OF THE LORD CAME UPON THEM

Luke ii: 9

★ The small notes are customarily sung instead of the large ones.

[5] From *Eight Festival Choruses from The Messiah* — Handel-Krone (Kjos)

Lord shone round a-bout them, and they were sore a-fraid.

Luke ii: 10,11
SOPRANO

AND THE ANGEL SAID UNTO THEM (No. 15)

Moderato

Piano

And the an-gel said un-to them, "Fear not: for be-hold, I bring you good

tid-ings of great joy, Which shall be to all peo-ple, For un-to you is born this

day in the cit-y of Da-vid a Sav-ior, which is Christ, the Lord."

★ These chords are played *after* the soprano has finished her phrase.

THE KEEPER (Excerpt) [6]

[6]From Our First Songs to Sing With Descants — Krone (Kjos)

CHAPTER EIGHT

CONDUCTING FIVES AND SEVENS

Music, to create harmony, must investigate discord.
—PLUTARCH.

Conducting Five-beat Measure.

Five-beat measure is rather common in pre-Bach choral music, and in modern music. Conductors beat the measure in various manners, but perhaps the easiest way for the young conductor to think of this meter is as a combination of three beats plus two, or of two plus three, depending upon how the music is written. Modern composers often put in dotted bars to indicate this.

Measures divided three plus two may be conducted as in Fig. 20. Make the fourth beat of *A* smaller than the first so that there can be no doubt as to which is the first beat of the measure.

Measures divided two plus three may be conducted as in Fig. 21. Make the third beat of *A* smaller than the first so that there can be no confusion as to which is the first beat of the measure.

Practice *Vainamoinen's Gift*[1] page 53.

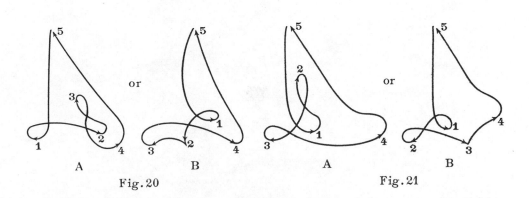

Five-beat measure. (3 plus 2)

Five-beat measure. (2 plus 3)

Fig. 20   Fig. 21

A Mighty Fortress, page 76, is also good for 5/4 practice.

[1] From *Songs of Sweden and Finland*—B. Krone and Ostlund (Kjos).

Conducting Seven-beat Measure.

Seven-beat measure is less frequently encountered. It may be thought of as four beats plus three, or three plus four, depending upon how the music has been written. As in five-beat measure, the composer or arranger often indicates the division of the measure by a dotted bar.

Four plus three may be conducted as in Fig. 22; three plus four as in Fig. 23. Be careful that the second down beat is not as strong as the first beat of the measure. Try the *Minstrel's Song*,[2] page 54.

Seven-beat measure.   Seven-beat measure.
(4 plus 3)   (3 plus 4)

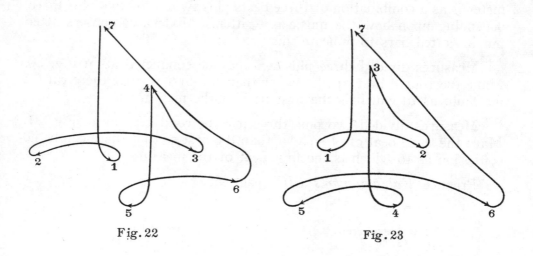

Fig. 22   Fig. 23

---

[2] From *Songs of Sweden and Finland*—B. Krone and Ostlund (Kjos).
Holst's *How Mighty Are the Sabbaths* (Unison) (G. Schirmer Inc.) is also excellent practice for 7/4.

Vainamoinen's Gift [3]

Text adapted by
B.P.K.

Finnish Rune
Arr. by B. P. K.

[3]From Songs of Sweden and Finland — Krone and Östlund (Kjos)

Minstrel's Song [4]

Text adapted by
B. P. K.

Finnish Rune
Arr. by B. P. K.

1. I am a min-strel born to sing the songs of__ Bra - gi,*
2. Known to__ me the dark un-earth-ly mag-ic__ treas - ure,
3. Let us__ tune the lute and sing our songs of__ glad - ness,

Born to__ sing he-ro-ic lay and an-cient__ sa - ga.
Mag-ic__ runes and rhymes I chant to bring you__ pleas - ure.
Ne'er shall__ we for-get the rhymes to ban-ish__ sad - ness.

* Bragi Boddason, the oldest known skald, lived in Norway in the middle of the ninth century. Pronounce to rhyme with saga.

[4]From Songs of Sweden and Finland   Krone and Ostlund (Kjos)

CHAPTER NINE

METRIC RELATIONSHIPS

There is music wherever there is harmony,
order, or proportion.

—Sir Thomas Brown (1605-1682).

Since so much of any conductor's task is concerned with tempo and rhythm, it is important that he have a clear understanding of and feeling for rhythmic relationships. Most of our music since the eighteenth century has been *metered* or *measured* off in regularly recurring metrical groups or measures, so we shall consider first the rhythmic relationships within this type of music and then discuss briefly the problems of conducting irregular meters.

Simple and Compound Meters

There are only a few meters which a young conductor is likely to encounter, but there are certain rhythmic relationships between these meters which it is important that he understand, feel, and be able to impart to his group. Some of these relationships may be seen in Fig. 24.

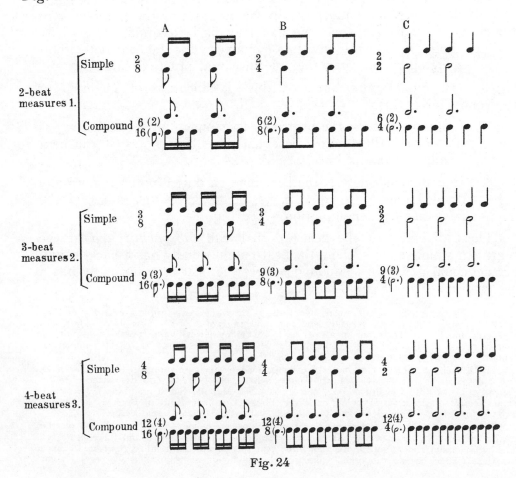

Fig. 24

The simple meters in each of the braces have this in common with the corresponding compound meters: meters 1 A, B, and C are all conducted two beats to a measure; meters 2 A, B, and C are all conducted three beats to a measure; meters 3 A, B, and C are all conducted four beats to a measure.

This may seem strange if you have learned that the upper number of the meter signature tells the number of beats in a measure and the lower number the kind of note that gets a beat. This rule holds good for simple meters, but not for compound ones.[1] In actual practice 6/8, for example, is *not* usually conducted six beats to a measure, however, but is conducted two beats to the measure. In this case a dotted quarter note, not an eighth note, gets a beat.

This fact brings out the *essential difference* between simple and compound meters, namely, that, the simple meters have a simple, "undotted" note for the beat note, e.g., an eighth, quarter, or half note. The compound meters have a dotted note for the beat note. Since there is no number that can be used to indicate a dotted note in the denominator of a compound meter signature, one way in which we could indicate the true character of these measures would be as we have done in parentheses after each of the compound meters in Fig. 24. Of course, if any of the compound meters were conducted slowly enough so that there were as many beats in the measure as the numerator of the signature indicated, then that meter would be a simple meter, with a simple note (a sixteenth, eighth, or quarter) for the beat note. This is the exception rather than the rule in actual practice, however.

The functional importance of this classification of meters[2] for the conductor is this:

1. In simple meters, the beat note (a simple, "undotted" note) is normally divided into *two* equal parts, i.e., notes of the next smaller denomination. See Fig. 24.

2. In compound meters, the beat note (a dotted note) is normally divided into *three* equal parts, i.e., *three simple notes* of the next smaller denomination. See Fig. 24.

These divisions of the beat we shall call the *background* of the beat. In simple meters, then, the beat note normally has a background of *two* equal notes; in compound meters the beat note normally has a background of *three* equal notes.

---

[1] A rule for explaining *all* meter signatures is this: *the meter signature is the product of the number of beats in a measure and the numerical value of the beat note.* Thus, 4/4 = 4 (the number of beats per measure) x 1/4 (the numerical value of the beat note, a quarter note). Similarly, 6/8 = 2 (the number of beats per measure) x 3/8 (the numerical value of a dotted quarter note).

The numerical values of all notes are determined by their relationship to a *whole note,* e.g., a dotted half note = 3/4 of a whole note, a half note = 1/2, a dotted quarter = 3/8, a quarter = 1/4, a dotted eighth = 3/16, and so on. See Melville Smith and Max T. Krone— *Fundamentals of Musicianship* (Witmark and Sons), Complete Edition, Book I, pp. 36, 37 and 93, for a more detailed explanation of note values and meter signatures.

[2] You will find also another classification of. meters in some texts, one based on the number of beats in the measure. In this classification, measures of two and three beats are called *simple,* and meters with more than three beats per measure are called *compound.* Since this classification has no functional value for the conductor or performer, we see no point in using it.

In order to *feel* this difference, conduct two-beat measure while you count aloud "one-ta, two-ta" for each measure, then continue beating two-beat measure while you count "one-ta-ta, two-ta-ta" for each measure. Shift back and forth in this counting of the background of simple and compound meters until you can *feel* the difference in background in your arm, without counting aloud. You may find it helpful at first to actually divide your beat into two or three parts as you count. The important thing, however, is to get the *feeling* of the background and to be able to shift easily from one background to the other.

Of course, a simple note may be divided into more equal parts than two, as can be seen in Fig. 25.

Equal Divisions of the Beat in Simple Meters

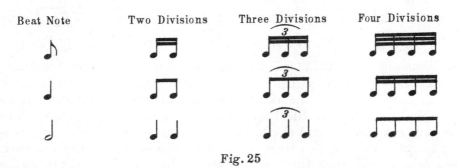

Fig. 25

Notice, however, that the less common divisions of the beat, the triplets, require a *3* above the notes. A division of four parts is an equal division into two parts of each *half* of the beat. Notice also that divisions of *two* and *three* parts are indicated with the same kind of note.

Similarly, a dotted note may be divided into other than three equal parts as is indicated in Fig. 26.

Equal Divisions of the Beat in Compound Meters

Fig. 26

Notice here that the less common divisions of the beat, the *duolets or duplets* and the *quartolets* or *quadruplets,* require either a *2* or *4* above the simple notes, or else the notes must be dotted. Notice especially that a dotted note may be divided into two or four equal dotted notes,[3] just as a simple note may be divided into two or four simple notes.

Practice making a counterclockwise circle with your left hand while you count two equal divisions of the beat. Do the same with three and four equal divisions. Be sure that the divisions that you count mark off equal spaces around the circle. Always hold each note for its *full* value, that is, until the beginning of the next note. Amateur musicians always need to be cautioned about this. They sing or play a note for half or three-quarters of its value and *think* they have given it its full value. There is always, therefore, a certain amount of "daylight" between every two notes. A true *legato* phrase is not possible under such conditions.

In counting threes, you may find yourself counting [♪♪♩] instead of [♪♪♪]. Once you have established the ability to *feel* any of these divisions accurately and without hesitation, you have the foundation for reading practically any rhythmic combination of notes. Figs. 27 and 28 show the derivation of various rhythmic patterns from equal divisions of the beat into three and four parts, and how these patterns may be read rhythmically.[4] The rhythmic counting indicated in these two figures uses the *beat* as the unit, not the measure. Every *beat* would, therefore, be counted, "One", and the divisions of the beat counted as indicated in the figures.

Patterns derived from [♪♪♪] **in 6/8 meter (or** [♪♪♪ (3)] **in 2/4 meter):**

1.

♪   ♪   ♪

Count: 1,   2,   3

3.

♪   [♩♩]   or   ♪   ♩

Count: 1   2———   1   2———
(one   two - oo)

2.

[♩♩]   ♪ or ♩   ♪

Count: 1———   3   1———   3
(wu - un   three)

4.

♪   ♪♪♪ or   ♪.   ♪♪

Count: 1——— ta 3   1——— ta 3
(wu - un ta three)

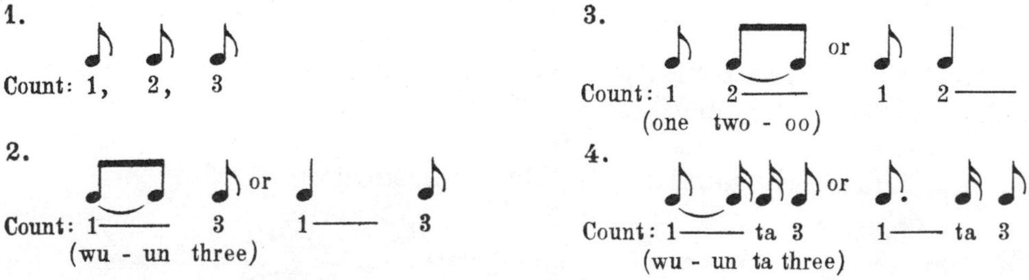

Fig. 27

---

[3] If this puzzles you, work out the relationship of Fig. 26 mathematically, for yourself. For example, a ♩·| is a 3/8 note (see the footnote, p. 56) ; ♪· a 3/16 note. Therefore, a ♩· equals two ♪· i.e. 3/8 = 2x3/16. Similarly, a ♩· = ♪·♪·♪·♪· (4 x 3/32).

[4] For a more detailed analysis of these rhythmic problems see *Fundamentals of Musicianship*, Smith-Krone, Witmark & Sons, Complete Edition, Book I, pp. 8-22, 35-54, 87-100, and in Book II, pp. 66-87. The rhythmic exercises in these two volumes provide valuable training for the conductor.

Patterns derived from ♩♩♩♩ , as in 2/4 meter:

Fig. 28

Practice reading these patterns rhythmically until you can shift from one to the other without hesitation. Notice the difference between 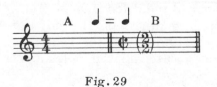 The former is often carelessly performed so that it sounds like the latter. Write out the patterns in Fig. 27 with a dotted eighth note as the beat note, and again with a dotted half note as the beat note. Write out the patterns of Fig. 28 with a half note as the beat note, and again with an eighth note as the beat note.

Changes in Meter.

Besides the relationship of simple and compound meters which we have just discussed, there are other relationships which the conductor must learn to sense and react to immediately. These relationships arise from changes in meter within a composition.

1. If in a composition there is a change of meter signature, it is usually assumed, unless otherwise indicated, that the time value of notes in the first section will remain the same in the second section. Frequently the composer, just to be safe, will indicate this thus:

Fig. 29

This means that the quarter note will get the same amount of time in section B as in section A. The *beat* in section B (half note) will, of course, be twice as slow as the *beat* of section A (quarter note).

Practice this at first by starting with four beats, then gradually make the second and third beats smaller and smaller until the second beat becomes merely a pause at the end of the down beat, and the third beat is merged with the up beat to make the second beat of the 2/2 measure.

To go from two or four beats to the measure, make a little pause in each of the two beats at the place where the curve of the "cane handle" begins. See Fig. 30. Then, at the time of the pause on one of the down beats, swing out to the left for the second beat of 4/4, and complete the beats of the 4/4 measure. After this transition becomes natural, practice conducting one measure with four and the next with two beats throughout an entire song.

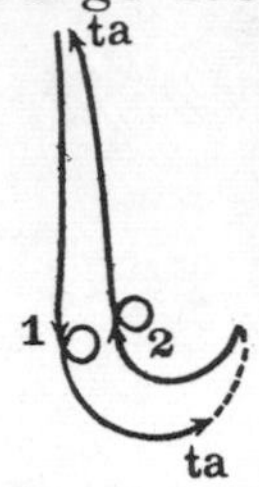

Fig. 30

Carmencita,[5] page 64, is a good song to practice for this type of meter change. Conduct the first four measures four beats to the measure as indicated. At (17) change to *alla breve* (¢), although it is not so indicated in the meter signature. There is a swing to the melody at (17) which makes this natural. Then too, the quarter note triplets will be much easier for conductor and chorus if he is conducting in 2/2 rather than in 4/4. At (20) change back to 4/4. Practice these changes from four beats to two, then back to four, until the transition can be made gracefully and easily.

Sometimes a composition may be written in 4/4, but because of the nature of the music itself, it is evident that it is better to conduct it as 2/2. *These Things Shall Be,* page 16, is an example of this. The predominance of half notes throughout the song would suggest to you that your choir would probably sing it more smoothly and phrase it more musically if you conduct it in 2/2. Try it both ways.

The same thing is true of *A Mighty Fortress Is Our God,* page 76. Here the possibility of either 4/4 or 2/2 is indicated in the meter signature. It will be easier for you to conduct the changes of meter in this song at first if you conduct the 4/4 measures in fours. But as soon as you have gained command of the meter changes, conduct these 4/4 measures as 2/2, and you will discover a freedom and flow to the phrases that is much more difficult to attain if you beat four beats for the 4/4 measures.

2. If, however, the composer had indicated ♩ = ♩ in Fig. 29, the amount of time given the *beat* in section B (half note) would be exactly the same as the time given the beat of section A (quarter note). In such a case, all the notes of section B

---

[5] From *Songs to Sing With Descants* (Kjos). Also published separately.

[6] From *Our First Songs to Sing With Descants* (Kjos).

[7] From *Great Songs of Faith*—B. and M. Krone (Kjos). The *Gloria Patri* has been arranged as an extended hymn in this collection and provides excellent practice for this type of meter change. *Praise to the Lord* in the same book is an interesting study for an alternation. of 3/4 and 6/4 meters.

[8] Thomas Morley's *Sing We and Chant It,* edited by the author (M. Witmark & Sons), is another good example of a song with phrases of 3/4, 3/2 and 3/4 meters.

would be performed twice as fast as similar notes in section A. This type of meter change does not usually cause the conductor much difficulty since the value of the beat note remains the same. *Stodola Pumpa*[6], page 62, is a song of this type.

Another interesting example of the first kind of meter change is found frequently in sixteenth- and seventeenth-century madrigals and motets, in which a phrase will sometimes consist of a measure of 3/4, a measure of 3/2 and then another measure of 3/4. The example from Palestrina's *Gloria Patri,*[7] page 67, is typical of this kind of meter change.[8] In conducting a phrase of this kind, this suggestion may be helpful: first, conduct the 3/2 measure with divided beats, thus:

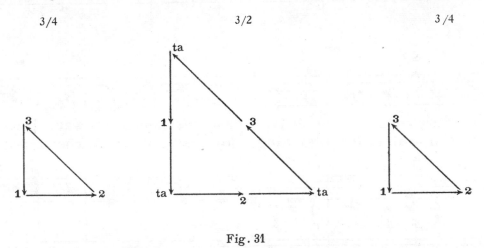

Fig. 31

Each of the *divisions* of the beats of the 3/2 measure represents a quarter note and will therefore receive as much time as each of the *beats* of the 3/4 measures. After this shift from one meter to the other becomes more automatic, discontinue the division of the beats of the 3/2 measure and make each beat a long, graceful stroke as in Fig. 32. This will hold the phrase together and give it a beautiful *legato*.

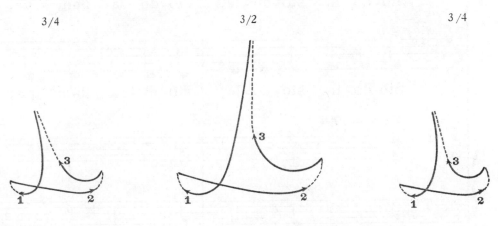

Fig. 32

STODOLA PUMPA (Excerpt) [9]

Czech

Come, walk with me, A - cross the fields to - day,
Come, dance with me, There's mu-sic in the air,

Sing - ing a song to pass the hours a - way. Hey!
Fid - dles are play - ing, joy is ev - 'ry - where. Hey!

Spoken

Twice as fast

*Sto-do-la, sto-do-la, sto-do-la pum - pa,

Sto-do-la, sto-do-la, sto-do-la pum - pa,

Twice as fast

★ *Stodola,* (barn) *pumpa,* (pump) are two Czech words which we do not translate, because it is more fun to sing them this way.

[9]From Our First Songs to Sing With Descants — Krone (Kjos)

CARMENCITA (Excerpt) [10]

(13) But I love my Car-men-ci-ta, My red-haired Cas-ti-llian
Chi-qui-llo no di-gus e-so, Que tu ma-dre va a pe-

rose, (17) The sweet-heart of all To-le-do The
gar, Mi ma-dre a mi-no me pe-ga, Cuan-

(20) love-li-est flow'r that grows. 2. The se-ño-ri-tas of
do di-go la ver-dad. DESCANT 2. *Ta ra la la la, Ta*

love-li-est flow'r that grows. 2. The se-ño-ri-tas of old Va-
do di-go la ver-dad. 2. *Ta ra la la la, Ta ra la*

old Va-len-cia Have tak-ing ways that will win you there, They're
ra la la la, Ta ra la la la la la la la, Pe-ro

len-cia Have ways that win you there, They're charm-ing
la la, Ta ra la la la la, Pe-ro e-sa

le - do, The love - li - est flow'r that grows.
pe - ga, Cuan - do di - go la ver - dad.
Ah

㊲

The señ - or - i - tas of Bar - ce - lo - na, With
Me gus - tan to - das, me gus - tan to - das, me

Car - men - ci - ta can - not com - pare, Her eyes are bright - er, her
gus - tan to - das en ge - ne - ral, pe - ro es - a ru - bia, pe - ro

laugh is light - er, There's no one like her an - y - where.
es - a ru - bia, pe - ro es - a ru - bia me gus - ta mas.

GLORIA PATRI (Excerpt)[11]

Palestrina

★ Glow-ree-ah Pah-tree ayt Fee-lee-oh, Ayt spee-ree-too-ee sahnk-toh.

[11]From Great Songs of Faith — Krone (Kjos).

CHAPTER TEN

OTHER METRIC RELATIONSHIPS

Music, when soft voices die,
Vibrates in the memory, . . .

—SHELLEY.

In Fig. 24, page 55, we observed a relationship between 2/4 and 6/8, since the number of *beats* in each meter was the same (two beats in each), but the *background* notes of the beats in the two meters were different in number, i.e., in 2/4,  , and in 6/8,

Shifting from 2/4 to 6/8 does not bother the conductor much so long as he gives the beat note the same amount of time in each of the two meters. All he has to do to feel the difference between the two is to count a background of threes for the beats of the 6/8 measures, and a background of twos for the beats of the 2/4 measures.

Another kind of change in meter for which the conductor must be prepared grows out of still another type of relationship between meters than those we have discussed. This is illustrated by Fig. 33 below.

Fig. 33

Here the relationship between 3/4 and 6/8 grows out of the fact that the number of *background* notes in each measure is the same (six eighth notes in each case) and all of the background notes receive the same amount of time. Both measures therefore occupy the same amount of time in performance. The number of *beats* in the two measures is different, however; there are three beats in the 3/4 measure and two beats in the 6/8 measure.

The alternation of 3/4 and 6/8 is a favorite Spanish and Latin American rhythmic practice. *The Silversmith*, page 72, is a good example and provides excellent practice since the measures alternate regularly (after the introduction) throughout the entire song.[1]

There are two problems involved for the conductor in conducting meter changes of this type:

1. To conduct the measure patterns correctly. This is a matter of practicing alternate two and three beats until the process is automatic.

2. To change the time value of the *beats* in 3/4 so that the *measure* of 3/4 occupies exactly the same amount of time as the measure of 6/8. This will not be difficult if you start by counting the *background* of each beat, thus:

Repeat throughout song.

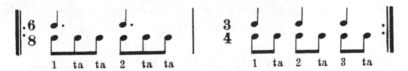

Fig. 34

Remember that in this relationship each of the *background* notes (eighth notes) gets the same amount of time. If you count the background notes regularly as in Fig. 34 and make your beats fit into the counting, your quarter notes (in 3/4) will automatically be enough faster than your dotted quarter note beats (in 6/8), that the two measures will occupy the same amount of time. As you get the feeling of the change, you can gradually drop out the mechanical counting of the background and concentrate on the more musical flow of the beats.

Irregular meter. Most of the composed music up to and well into the seventeenth century was vocal, since instruments were quite crude, and most of the composers made their living as court or chapel choirmasters and composers. Furthermore, since the Church wished to keep all secular influences out of the service, music which suggested dancing, i.e., regularly metered music, was not considered good music for religious services.

The Church composers of the fifteenth, sixteenth, and early seventeenth centuries have therefore left us a wealth of beautiful choral music that scrupulously avoids regular meter and that is strangely disturbing at first to our rhythmic habit of starting in one meter and staying in it for at least a section if not the entire length of the composition. Sometimes composers or arrangers of later times have dis-

---

[1] The printed edition of this song in *Spanish and Latin American Songs,* arranged by the Krones (Kjos), is scored in 3/8. Conducted thus, it presents no problem for even an inexperienced conductor. The true rhythm of the song, however, is indicated in the excerpt given here, and the trained, musical conductor would conduct it throughout in alternate 6/8 and 3/4 even though it is barred in 3/8.

The following Latin American songs offer interesting opportunities for practice of this device:

Cielito Lindo—Kjos Octavo No. 1029 (SATB) or 1201 (SSA).
Chiapanecas—Kjos Octavo No. 1021 (SATB) or 1202 (SSA).
Rio, Rio—Belwin Inc. Octavo No. 621 (SSA).

torted the rhythm of these early works to make them fit into regular meters, much as popular song writers distort classic melodies today to make them fit into dance meters.

Such was the case with Luther's great hymn, *A Mighty Fortress Is Our God,* which appears in most hymnals today in a square-toed, 4/4 meter. The original form, in Hassler's harmonization, given on pages 76 to 78, will seem strange at first, but once you have learned to shift easily from one meter to another, and to conduct and sing *through the phrase* instead of from one measure bar to the next, you will discover a rhythmic freshness and virility which is quite thrilling, and which is lost in the distorted 4/4 version. See the suggestion concerning conducting this song on page 60.

Incidentally, this is an excellent review of all the meters you have studied so far. If you get mixed up in your patterns or lose your place, conduct down beats until you find yourself again. This is a good rule to follow in all your conducting.

Conducting Sixteenth-Century Polyphonic Music

In *A Mighty Fortress* the four voices move together in the same rhythm most of the time; it is predominantly *harmonic* in character. Most of the choral music of the fifteenth and sixteenth centuries, however, was *polyphonic* rather than harmonic. The emphasis was upon independent voice parts rather than upon chords underlying a given melody. There are suggestions of this independent voice treatment in *A Mighty Fortress.*

Composers of this period did not use bar lines at regular intervals as has been done since the seventeenth century, and the singers of that day read their parts from individual partbooks, without ever seeing a complete score, so they did not need bars to help them keep their places with the other parts. They just gave the same kinds of notes the same amount of time throughout and accented their melody as the words and melody line indicated without worrying about an accent every two, three, or four beats as we do.[2]

As editors began to publish these choruses in full score, they added bars at regular intervals to make it easier for the singers to keep their places. Since the voice parts were originally written in irregular meter, and since each part was rhythmically independent of the others, these added bar lines obscure the original rhythms, and in spite of ourselves we tend to sing an accent every time we cross the measure bar, an accent which the composer usually did not intend. It was for this reason that the editions made by the author have been barred with dotted bars which extend *between* the staves at more or less regular intervals, but which cross the staff of any one part only when the rhythm of that part calls for these bars. *O Bone Jesus,* page 74, is a

---

[2] See Smith-Krone—*Fundamentals of Musicianship* (Witmark), Complete Edition, Vol. II, page 73 ff.; Fellowes—*English Madrigal Composers* (Oxford), Chap. XI; and Morris—*Sixteenth Century Contrapuntal Technique* (Oxford).

very simple example. Here the meter changes occur for the most part simultaneously in all the voice parts. You will notice several places however where individual parts have metrical patterns which lie across the pattern of the other voices.

In conducting music of this period it is evident that the conductor cannot beat all the meters that occur in the different voices simultaneously. There are two ways of solving this problem. One is to conduct the meters indicated by the dotted bars which extend between the staves; the other, to conduct every beat as a down-beat and to indicate the entrances and points of prominence of each part. In either case, each section will need to practice its own part until it can sing it without being thrown off by the others.

Other editors have since adopted this device,[3] but most of the available editions are regularly barred.[4] It is important, therefore, that the conductor study such scores carefully, playing or singing through each voice part, marking its real meter with some system of his own so that he may help his singers to get the true rhythm of their parts in as short a time as possible. There is such a feeling of freedom and achievement that comes to a choir that masters one or two of these choruses. It gives a new vitality to their singing of regularly metered music also, just as the haunting, modal beauty of much sixteenth-century music gives a new tonal thrill, and as the pure vowels of the Latin text serve as a perfect medium for vocalizing.[5]

[3] See especially the editions of Paul Boepple, published by the Music Press, N. Y., and Hans David—*The Art of Polyphonic Song* (G. Schirmer).

[4] The following choruses (SATB), edited by the author, are suitable for use with school choruses:

Wm. Byrd—*Agnus Dei*	Carl Fischer Inc.
Wm. Byrd—*Ave Maria* (published without bars so that students of choral technics may experiment with barring, themselves)	M. Witmark & Sons
Wm. Byrd—*Ave Verum Corpus*	M. Witmark & Sons
M. Ingegneri—*Tenebrae Factae Sunt*	M. Witmark & Sons
Thos. Morley—*Sing We and Chant It*	M. Witmark & Sons
G. Palestrina—*Adoramus Te*	M. Witmark & Sons
G. Palestrina—*Gloria Patri*	Neil Kjos Music Co.
G. Pitoni—*Adoramus Te*	M. Witmark & Sons
T. Vittoria—*Ave Maria*	M. Witmark & Sons

[5] See Max T. Krone, *The Chorus and Its Conductor,* Kjos Music Co., for Latin pronunciation (Chap. V) and for a more detailed treatment of the choral forms of the sixteenth and seventeenth centuries (Chap. VIII).

The Silversmith [6]
(Excerpt)

Spanish Folk Song
(Andalusia)
Arr. by B. & M.K.

Tell me, sil - ver - smith, oh tell me, How much sil - ver would you need? Just to frame a kiss so ten - der, Can you frame a kiss __ in -

Can you frame a kiss

O Bone Jesu*

S. A. T. B.

Edited by M.T.K.

GIOVANNI PIERLUIGI
da PALESTRINA

★ Oh *bo*-nay *yay*-zoo! *mee*-zay-*ray*-ray *noh*-bees, *kwee-ah* cray-*ah*-stee nohs; too *ray*-day-*mee*-stee nohs *sahn*-gwee-nay *too*-oh *pray*-tsee-oh-*sees*-see-moh.

O blessed Jesus, have mercy upon us; Thou who hast created us and redeemed us by Thy most precious blood.

A Mighty Fortress Is Our God

Mixed Voices

Second stanza by Max T. Krone

Martin Luther(1483-1546)
Harmonized by Hans Leo Hassler (1564-1612)
Edited by M.T.K.

★ Luther's use of this 3/4 – 5/4 pattern breaks the monotony of a straight 4/4 meter in a decidedly "modern" manner. Give the quarter notes the same amount of time throughout.

⁷Published separately by Kjos Music Co.   Ed. No. 811

★ The accentuation of the tenor measure must be 2-3
★★ The sopranos here have a 5/4 - 3/4 pattern, and should accentuate it that way.

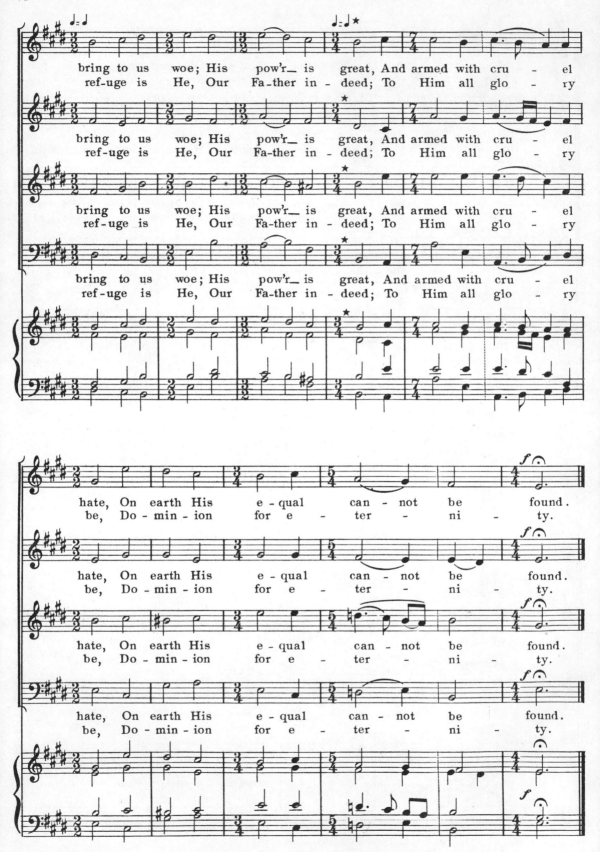

CHAPTER ELEVEN

COMMMUNITY AND ASSEMBLY SINGING

For most of us, music is primarily something to be experienced, not to be studied; to be enjoyed, not to be analyzed; a pleasurable experience motivated from within, not "lessons" arbitrarily imposed from without.

Community singing. More and more the school music teacher is becoming a community music leader, especially in smaller towns and cities. This is a healthy development and provides many opportunities for the building up of community instrumental and choral groups that can serve the players and singers who are being trained in our school groups. It also provides opportunity for the school conductor to make a contribution to his community through leadership in community singing.

Community singing has been associated so much with periods of stress, such as the two World Wars, and has often been so poorly organized and carried on that musicians have come to look down upon it as something with little or no musical values and hence beneath their dignity and outside the pale of their activities. From the purely selfish standpoint alone, however, it would be wise to have more taxpayers interested in our music program. The "Community Sing" provides one such opportunity to reach this group.

We are likely also to forget the slogan of the Music Educators National Conference, "Music for *every* child, every child *for* music," and to be concerned only with those children (and in the community, those adults) who are talented enough to "make" the band, orchestra, and choir—usually a group of from 10 to 25 per cent of the high school population. There is a great challenge to us in this situation to keep in touch with the 75 to 90 per cent who are not in special groups in high school or who do not participate in musical activities as adults, and to provide a stimulating *musical* experience for them in the assembly or community sing.

Since there are several good books[1] devoted to the organization and carrying on of community singing, we shall only outline briefly some of the important factors in the conducting of such a "sing."

---

[1] A. A. Zanzig, *Community and Assembly Singing,* National Recreation Ass'n., N. Y.,
B. Playground and Recreation Ass'n., *Community Music,* C. C. Birchard, Boston;
C. S. H. Frieswyk, *Forty Approaches to Informal Singing,* National Recreation Ass'n., N. Y.,
D. K. S. Clark, *Community Singing and the Community Chorus,* National Bureau for the Advancement of Music, N. Y.

The words. Have the words available, through either song slides[2] or word sheets in the hands of the singers[3]. This is very important. Very few people can remember more than a line or two of a song.

Good accompanist. Choose a good accompanist, preferably one who does not need to use music and who can improvise interesting, rhythmic accompaniments in several keys. This is important, because there is no one source for all the songs you will want to use and your group will want to sing, so your pianist will be continually looking for something that is somewhere else. And, in the second place, most songs are pitched too high for community singing, and people do not enjoy singing out of a comfortable range. From c' to d'' is the best range for community songs. And, finally, your pianist should be able to play different types of accompaniments, from full chords to delicate arpeggios, depending on the character of the song and the need of the singers for support on the melody.

If you can not find a pianist who possesses all these attributes, do the best you can, but go over with him carefully all the songs you are going to use and be sure he has the music in the right key, and can play it with certainty and flexibility. If you have to drag him along, you are lost.

The program. Choose an interesting and varied program. Probably the two chief reasons why community sings fail are, first, the conductor's inability to have a good time with his group and, second, his failure to give enough attention to building interesting programs. We shall consider the matter of conducting community singing shortly; a word now about the program.

The songs listed on page 91 are grouped under several headings, which will suggest to you a variety of types of songs which may be used. Select a number of different types for each program. Keep in mind, too, the importance of changes of mood and tempo. Do not sing too many lusty, vigorous songs in succession, or too many slow, sentimental ones. Work in a "stunt" song occasionally, such as *My Hat*[4] to give the singers a chance to smile or laugh, as well as to move around a little or to stand up.

Sometimes a group of songs built around a central theme, such as marching songs of the nations of the world, will add interest to a program. Such a group might include:

American: *Yankee Doodle, Battle Hymn of the Republic* (see descant, Fig. 39, page 83), *Dixie, Marine's Hymn, Over There, When Johnny Comes Marching Home, Caisson Song.*

---

[2] May be procured from The Sims Visual Music Co., Quincy, Ill., or may be made with materials obtainable from school supply companies. See the note on copyrights, on page 90, however.

[3] See page 90.

[4] See page 92.

English: *Hiking Song*[5], *Onward Christian Soldiers, British Grenadiers , I've Got Six-pence.*

French: *The Marseillaise, The Fighting French (Regiment of Sambre and Meuse and Marseillaise*[5]*).*

Chinese: *Song of the Volunteers* (Chee Lai[6]).

Negro: *Lift Your Voices* (National Hymn)—R. Johnson[7]

New songs: Learn at least one new song each time. Any song of the list on page 91 can be learned by rote in ten minutes at the most. If a song requires more than that, it probably is not a good one for community singing. Your singers will enjoy mostly singing songs they already know, but we all like to learn a new one occasionally.

Provide for requests. Preferably these should be written down and turned in at one meeting to be sung at the next. This will give you a chance to plan a unified program including the requests, will not put your pianist "on the spot," and will give you a chance to have the words available.

Old songs rejuvenated. Brighten up some old song with a new treatment:

1. **A descant.** A simple descant (counter-melody), which may be used with any song that can be harmonized with tonic, subdominant, and dominant chords only, may be constructed from these tetrachords:

   do ti la so   fa mi re do   so so la ti
      I   IV   V

For example, with *The Marine's Hymn*:

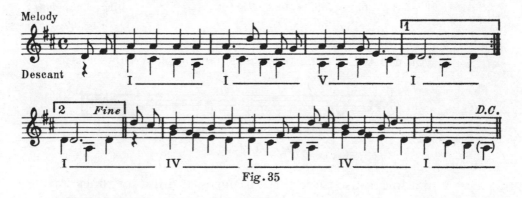

Fig. 35

---

[5] Arr. by the Krones (Neil A. Kjos Co.).
[6] Pub. by Carl Fischer Inc.
[7] Pub. by Edward Marks Co.

The descant may be sung with "Tramp, tramp, tramp, tramp," all the way through, or you may make up simple words, such as this "Navy" version:

> N-A-V-Y, N-A-V-Y, N-A-V-Y men (or Waves) are we
>
> (repeat),
>
> One-two-three-four, N-A-V-Y (repeat)
>
> N-A-V-Y, N-A-V-Y, N-A-V-Y men (or Waves) are we.

You can teach such a descant very quickly by having your singers sing the pattern for each chord as you hold up one, four, or five fingers. Then as they sing the song, all they need to do is to watch your finger signals. Let them all sing the descant, with the help of the piano first, then divide them into two groups, one for the melody and one for the descant. Of course, you want to be sure you know when to use each chord! *Camptown Races* lends itself nicely to this treatment; you will think of others.

You can easily teach a simple descant such as many of those in *Our First Songs to Sing with Descants* or *Songs to Sing with Descants* by rote.[10]

For any short round, such as *Are You Sleeping,* which is harmonized with only one chord, you can make up a simple descant using tones of the chord, which may be sung over and over during the round, for example:

Oh, John! Oh, John! Oh, John!   or   Ding, ding, dong.

Fig. 36   Fig. 37

or you can use a scale pattern, sung, or played on bells:

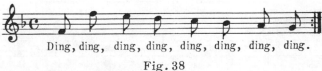

Ding, ding, ding, ding, ding, ding, ding, ding.

Fig. 38

You also can use these three patterns at different times during the singing of the round, or use them all simultaneously. Try making up simple descants yourself, like this one for the Refrain of *Battle Hymn of the Republic*[11]:

---

10 Try these from *Our First Songs* (Kjos): *Sing, Sing, Together; Row, Row, Row; How Sweet Is Our Singing; Hot Cross Buns; Lovely Evening; Hickory, Dickory, Dock; London Bridge; An Autumn Round; Stodola Pumpa; Merrily We Roll Along.* From *Songs to Sing* (Kjos), try *Three Blind Mice* and *Come Let Us Work.*

11 See the descant arrangement of this song in *Great Songs of Faith*, Krones (Kjos).

Fig. 39

2. Vocal Chordal Accompaniments:

Put this diagram on the blackboard where everyone can see it.

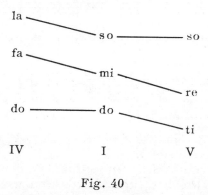

Fig. 40

a) **Blocked chords.** Everyone likes to harmonize, and this is an easy way to do it. Divide the singers into three groups, the lowest voices sustaining the root, the middle voices the third, and the high voices the fifth of the tonic chord. Point to the syllable each part is to sing, in the diagram (Fig. 40). When the chord sounds in tune, practice changing from tonic to subdominant to tonic; from tonic to dominant to tonic; and from tonic to subdominant to dominant and back again to tonic. Syllables may be used in the blending exercise, but when the melody starts, have the group change to a hum, or to some neutral syllable. The melody may be sung by a soloist, a selected group, or the choir or glee club.

When the large group is accustomed to changing chords, they will no longer need to watch the blackboard but can keep their eyes on you. You can guide them by holding up one finger when you want the tonic chord, four fingers for the subdominant, and five for the dominant. No piano accompaniment is necessary, so this is a good device to use if you are called on to lead singing somewhere where there is no piano.

A few of the songs which are effective when accompanied in this manner are: *Swanee River, Home on the Range, There's Music in the Air,* and Brahms' *Lullaby.*

Sometimes it is effective to have the accompaniment group *sing the words* on their tones instead of humming, as a climax or at the end of a song. For instance, in *Aunt Dinah's Quilting Party,* humming may be used up to the last phrase of the refrain, and then the words may be sung, the chordal group singing the same rhythm as the melody. See Fig. 41.

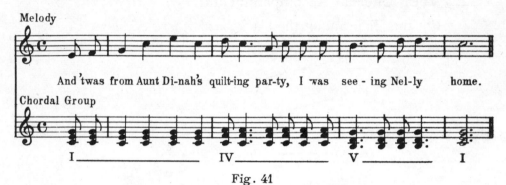

Fig. 41

b) **Broken chords.** For some types of songs you may want to break up the chords and use only certain intervals as an accompanying counter-melody. Brahms' *Lullaby,* for instance, lends itself to this type of treatment.[12]

1) Begin with an introduction on the tonic chord, using the well-known rhythmic figure:

5   3   5   or   <u>so</u> - <u>mi</u> - <u>so</u>

2) Practice from the diagram, Fig. 40, using the two top tones of the triads in the rhythm of (1) as an accompaniment to the melody.

3) When the group is going along well, drop the syllables and sing, "Lul-la-by."

c) **Banjo effects.** For songs like *Oh Susanna* and *Dixie,* you can easily teach a banjo type of accompaniment, using Fig. 40. The men and boys can sing the first beat of the measure (or every other measure), using the lower notes of the chords and singing "plunk" with nasal quality. The girls can use the upper notes of the chords, singing after-beats, with nasal "plink, plank, plank" or "plinkity, plank, plank."

---

12 See page 24 for a chordal treatment like the one suggested here.

3. **Rounds.** Everybody enjoys singing rounds. The traditional way of using them is for the leader to divide the audience into the proper number of groups, depending on whether
the song is a three-, four-, or eight-part round. He then de-
cides how many times the round should be sung through com-
pletely, indicates which group is to begin first, and sometimes
suggests certain dynamic effects for each section to observe.
At the completion of the round, the sections either drop out
one at a time, or the whole group comes to a complete stop on
the chord when the leader gives the signal at the end of a phrase.

Here are some interesting and effective devices for making
the old rounds a little more exciting and challenging to a group.
Take the Russian round *Hey, Ho!* for example:

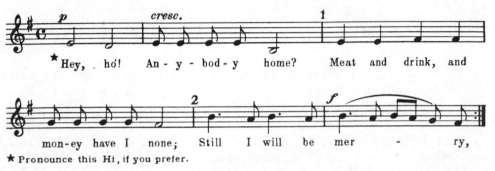

★ Pronounce this Hi, if you prefer.

Fig. 42

a) Instead of beginning "cold," start with an introduction
of some sort, for example:

Fig. 43

An even easier introduction and also an effective one is to
use the characteristic interval, *la-so,* beginning softly, and
repeating more loudly with each entering voice:

Fig. 44

b)   Just as it is effective to have a simple introduction to a
round, it is effective also to have a "coda" to end it.   This,
too, can be built on a chord or from part of the melodic
pattern of the round.   For instance:

Fig. 45

You can make up an introduction and coda for *Are You
Sleeping?* from Figs. 36 to 38.   Try singing *Are You
Sleeping?* with *Three Blind Mice* also.

Hand signals.   Use hand signals to indicate different kinds of
performance.   For example, hand open and held over head means
"sing"; hand closed and at chest level means "hum"; pointing downward with index finger, "whistle."   This is a good way to keep everyone's eyes on you, and everybody enjoys it.   It is also useful if you
have a soloist do a phrase or section of a song—you can give the *hum*
signal and get a humming accompaniment for the soloist without say-
ing a word.

Competition.   Play off groups against each other: men against
women; balcony against those on the main floor; right side against
left.   Each side may take turns singing stanzas or, better still, use
the hand signals, the right hand for the men, the left for the women,
and so on.

Surprise.   Have some special surprise feature for each meeting;
a soloist, trio, quartet, reader, comedy sketch, a group of folk dancers,
a reel of movies, and so on.   Draw on your school and community
resources.

Conducting.   It is often difficult for the conductor of picked
groups to adjust himself to conducting community singing because
he tries to make a rehearsal of it and seeks the same kind of perfec-
tion of performance as with his choir.   It is hard for him to realize
that the essential element in a successful "sing" is spontaneous enjoy-
ment, not a finished performance.   These people are singing *for their
own satisfaction,* not for that of an audience, just as folk singers of
all time have gathered around one of their number with a guitar, a

dulcimer, a ukelele, a banjo, a reed organ, or a piano, and have sung their hearts out because it was good to do so.

The situation is more formal with a larger group, and the leader becomes more than merely an accompanist for their singing; however, the more he is able to identify himself with his group and to enjoy himself with them, the more likelihood there is of success. *That is one reason why experienced leaders get as close to their singers as possible, and avoid standing on a platform or stage away from the group.*

Since the community song director should try to be and feel like one of the group rather than a musical dictator, it follows that his conducting should be as simple as possible. This does not mean that you should discard all you have learned about conducting technic simply because your singers do not know what the conventional patterns mean. You can still retain these patterns, but superimpose the *rhythm of the melody* onto them. Thus, in *America*:

Fig. 46

The length of the lines under the letters indicates the approximate, proportional length of the beats. Thus, in the second measure, the down beat is held for a beat and a half, and the beat to the right comes with the eighth note and is correspondingly short.

Try conducting the *Star Spangled Banner* in this way.

Fig. 47

Here, in the second measure, the down beat is held for two beats, and two up beats are given in rhythm with the dotted eighth and sixteenth notes, because it is hard for most people to remember whether these two notes are even or jerky.[13]

---

[13] It may help you to remember where these "jerky rhythms" occur in the *Star Spangled Banner* if you note that the figures *mi-re-do, la-ti-do,* and *so-mi-do* are always "jerky". The key of *A* or *Ab* is best for community singing.

With a song that everyone knows, it isn't necessary to conduct in the usual manner at all after you get them started, except perhaps at the beginning of phrases. Save your motions for some special dynamic effect, or for signals to hum or whistle. The more you conduct, the less you will seem like one of the group.

Assembly Singing

High school. What we have said about community singing applies equally to assembly singing in high school. Here, however, you have other opportunities for making the "sing" more interesting and varied. The orchestra may be used for accompaniments on some of the songs and for special numbers occasionally. The glee clubs, choir, and small ensembles may be used for special numbers also, or they may sing descants which they have learned in rehearsals to the melodies sung by the student body. Or they may sing a harmonization of a melody sung in unison by the other students.

The students may be seated by voice parts in order that some songs may be sung in harmony. In this case, a section of the orchestra may be assigned to play voice parts, each section standing behind or facing the voice part it is helping.

With certain types of songs (Mexican, South American, American cowboy, and so on), it is appropriate and effective to use percussion instruments as an accompaniment. These may be played by students who are not regular members of the orchestra, but who have a good sense of rhythm and are dependable. Such combinations as several drums of different sizes, maracas, and claves may be used on Cuban and Latin-American songs. Each type of instrument may take a typical rhythmic pattern and carry it throughout the song, or different combinations of instruments may be used on different sections of the song, in order to avoid monotony. Also, instruments typical of the ones used by these groups would be appropriate, e.g., guitar, violin, bass (and piano if necessary) for Mexican songs.

Popular songs. The question of whether to use popular songs always comes up in connection with assemblies. In the light of the nature and purposes of community singing, we can see no good reason for not using them, *among other types of songs.* Obviously, there are some popular songs that are vulgar, cheap, and of no musical or textual significance. Naturally, you would not use this type. On the other hand, you can undoubtedly name ten or a dozen songs that are and have been popular during the past five to ten years that have survived because they *are good* songs, some of them better and more interesting than a lot of songs in community song books.

You will find it an interesting experience to have a Request Box into which the students may put their requests for songs. Some will be for the two types of popular songs we have mentioned above. You will have to be the judge as to whether a song is of the first type and not appropriate. There will also be requests for songs that are of passing interest or which you feel are on the borderline. Schedule one or two such songs at the next sing, and see if they are requested again. In most cases you will find they are not.

Every generation must relive the experiences of the one before it, and must learn to form its own judgments on the basis of these experiences. In the case of songs for example, students need to hear and sing many kinds in order to have a proper perspective of values. Our job is to see that they have this opportunity. If we cannot give them an interesting experience singing songs *we* think are good ones, we can hardly blame them for wanting to sing the songs *they* think are interesting.

Junior high and elementary schools. What has been said in regard to assembly singing on the high school level is appropriate for junior high and grade school levels, also. The *approach* is the same, but the materials used will often differ. Choirs can be used for special effects and descants. Rounds may be treated in exactly the same manner. The use of chords may be applied just as easily at these levels as at the higher levels, if their use is gradual and *not forced*. As a matter of fact, this kind of procedure helps children to appreciate the value of some of the skills they have learned (such as the use of syllables).

Instrumental accompaniments may have to be confined to the use of simple instruments which the children can handle easily, such as bells, autoharps, recorders, or tonettes, and simple percussion instruments. Bells are effective on such songs as the round *Oh, How Lovely Is the Evening*. Autoharps are lovely accompaniment instruments for lullabies, home songs, and pioneer songs. Wind instruments can often be used to bolster up harmony parts or a descant, and percussion instruments are appropriate and effective: tambourines and gourds on certain types of Spanish, Italian, and Mexican songs; drums and flute on Indian songs; the woodblock on clock and pony songs; gong and drums on Oriental songs.

The elementary school assembly provides a fine opportunity for each classroom group to make a contribution of its own. In many school systems, there is a core of songs which is learned in each grade and kept in the children's repertory. The assembly is a good setting for the singing of these songs. Then, too, the older children may learn a harmonization or descant for some of these songs, which they can sing while the younger children sing the melody, thus giving the lower grades experience with part singing before they try it themselves.

The odor of pedagogy. Keep the odor of pedagogy out of the whole thing, no matter what age group you are working with. Your crowd does not want to be *taught,* they want to have a good time *with you*. But that does not mean that there can be no educational values in community singing. The skillful teacher can create a learning situation without the learner being aware that he is learning. The development of attitudes and of social values and social consciousness takes place best in such an environment. And community singing has a great deal to contribute in these fields.

The words of the kindly old minister, who always addressed his congregation thus before the first hymn of the day, "Now, all those that can, sing. The rest of us will make a joyful noise to the Lord," are very much to the point in community singing.

Suggested Songs

The following songs are suggested as a nucleus from which you can make up an interesting program that almost any group will enjoy singing. To it, of course, you can add songs of local or regional interest, school songs, and current popular songs.

The starred songs are copyright by other publishers and may not be reproduced (words or music) by anyone except the copyright owners or their assignees. The copyright law protects the owner of a copyright for two periods of twenty-eight years each, or fifty-six years in all. Copying of any copyright material by any process is a violation of this right. Music or words on which the copyright has expired (that is, if the copyright was first taken out more than fifty-six years ago) are said to be "in the public domain" and may be used by anyone. A new *arrangement* of the music, or a new translation of a foreign text, may be copyrighted by the arranger, translator, or their publisher, however, and this in turn is protected for another fifty-six years maximum. You may use the words of the songs preceded by a (K) in your own song sheets, provided they are used only with your own school or community group and are not sold. The words and melody of all the other songs in the list are in the public domain.

The code letters following each song title refer to the sources of the music as indicated in the following *Key to Symbols Used,* and the numbers indicate the page of the book in which the music occurs.

Key to Symbols Used:

BB—Blue Book of Favorite Songs
    Hall & McCreary Co.
CC—Christmas Carolers' Book—Kvamme
    Hall & McCreary Co.
CF—Carl Fischer Inc., N. Y.
FDT—From Descants to Trios—B.&M.K.
    (Kjos)
Fl—Flammer Music Co., N. Y.
FSTSWD—First Songs to Sing With
    Descants—B. P. Krone.
    Neil A. Kjos Co.
GSF—Great Songs of Faith—Krones
    (Kjos)
GS—G. Schirmer Inc., N. Y.
Kj-Octvo—Arrangements by B. & M.
    Krone
    Neil A. Kjos Co.
KOS—Keep on Singing—Clark
    Paull-Pioneer Music Co., N. Y.
LS—Living Songs—Gildersleeve & Smith
    Carl Fischer Inc.

NASB—New American Song Book
    Hall & McCreary Co.
S—Sing!
    C. C. Birchard Co., Boston
SA—Singing America—Zanzig
    C. C. Birchard Co.
SGN—Songs of the Gay Nineties
    Robbins Music Corp., N. Y.
STSWD—Songs to Sing With Descants
    —B. Krone
    Neil A. Kjos Co.
SWS—Songs We Sing
    Hall & McCreary Co.
TFB—Twice 55 Brown Book
    C. C. Birchard Co.
TFG—Twice 55 Green Book
    C. C. Birchard Co.
UFS—Universal Folk Songster—Botsford
    G. Schirmer Inc.
VSB—Victory Song Book
    Robbins Music Corp.

SONGS FOR COMMUNITY SINGS

Patriotic and Service Songs

AMERICA (BB 3) (KOS 126) (TFB 1) (LS 79) (NASB 62) (S 144) (SA 125)
AMERICA THE BEAUTIFUL (BB 7) (TFB 5) (KOS 126) (LS 80) (NASB 126) (S 143)
*ANCHORS AWEIGH (VSB)
  Copyright Robbins Music Corp.
*ARMY AIR CORPS SONG
  Copyright Carl Fischer Inc.
BATTLE HYMN OF THE REPUBLIC (BB 12) (TFB 94) (NASB 105) (GSF 43)
CAISSON SONG
DIXIE (BB 10) (TFB 62) (LS 85) (NASB 104) (S 60) (SA 123) (SWS 39)
*KEEP THE HOME FIRES BURNING (TFB 177—words only) Copyright Chappell & Co.
MARINE'S HYMN (NASB 127) (see p. 81).
*OVER THERE (VSB)
  Copyright Robbins Music Corp.
STAR SPANGLED BANNER (BB 4) (TFB 3) (KJOS 125) (LS 82) (NASB 65) (S 142) (SA 124)
WHEN JOHNNY COMES MARCHING HOME (Kj-octvo) (BB 18) (TFB 9) (NASB 111) (STSWD 38)
YANKEE DOODLE (BB 8) (TFB 95) (L 87) (NASB 63) (STSWD 18)

Rounds

ARE YOU SLEEPING? (BB 121) (TFB 10)
DO NOT WORRY (UFS)
HEY, HO, ANYBODY HOME? (see p. 85)
LITTLE TOM TINKER (BB 124) (SWS 115)
LOVELY EVENING (BB 70) (TFB 21)
O HOW SWEET IS OUR SINGING (SA 60)
SING, SING TOGETHER (FSTSWD 2)
THREE BLIND MICE (BB 119) (TFB 69) (STSWD 8)

Stephen Foster Songs

BEAUTIFUL DREAMER (BB 268) (KOS 27) (SWS 34)
CAMPTOWN RACES (LS 48) (S 56) (SWS 37)
JEANIE WITH THE LIGHT BROWN HAIR (SA 34)
MY OLD KENTUCKY HOME (BB 26) (TFB 22) (LS 43) (NASB 97) (SA 34a) (SWS 83)
O SUSANNA (BB 220) (LS 8) (NASB 103) (S 54)
OLD FOLKS AT HOME (BB 27) (TFB 16) (LS 39) (NASB 96) (S 58) (SA 33)
SOME FOLKS (Kj-octvo) (S 51) (SWS 71)

Spirituals and Southern Songs

CARRY ME BACK TO OLD VIRGINNY (BB 32) (TFB 112) (LS 15) (S 42) (SA 35a) (SWS 85)
K. CLIMBIN' UP THE MOUNTAIN (Kj-octvo) (FDT 10) Copyright M. T. K.
DEEP RIVER (BB 251) (TFG 67) (LS 23) (NASB 23) (SWS 40)
GO DOWN, MOSES (BB 97) (TFG 69)
K. JESUS WALKED THIS LONESOME VALLEY (GSF 41) Copyright M. T. K.
LIL LIZA JANE (NASB 31)
NOBODY KNOWS THE TROUBLE I'VE SEEN (BB 220) (TFG 71) (NASB 25)
SHORT'NIN' BREAD (LS 18) (S 70) (SWS 23)
SWING LOW, SWEET CHARIOT (BB 95) (TFB 48) (LS 21) (NASB 24)
K. TRAMPIN' (GSF 13) Copyright M. T. K.

Home

ALL THROUGH THE NIGHT (BB 41) (TFB 24) (LS 65) (NASB 151) (SA 64a)
BRAHMS' LULLABY (FDT 14) (BB 81) (TFG 19) (S 26) (p. 24 of this book)
*HOME ROAD—Carpenter (BB 134)
  Copyright G. Schirmer Inc.
HOME, SWEET HOME (BB 24) (TFB 23) (NASB 72)
SWEET AND LOW (BB 42) (TFB 25) (SWS 80)

Cheer-Up Songs

K. BOOM FA-DA-RA-LA (Kj-octvo)
  Copyright M.T.K.
K. CZECH DANCE SONG (STSWD 5) (Kj-octvo) Copyright B.P.K.
FUNICULI, FUNICULA (NASB 143) (BB 176) (SWS 42)
*I WANT TO BE HAPPY
  Copyright Music Publishers Holding Corp., N. Y.
*PACK UP YOUR TROUBLES (TFB 179—words only)
  Copyright Chappell & Co.
K. STODOLA PUMPA (FSTSWD 19)
  Copyright B.P.K.

Love Songs

ANNIE LAURIE (BB 39) (TFB 30) (LS 55) (NASB 92) (SA 63a)
*BELLS OF ST. MARY'S
  Copyright Chappell & Co.
*DOWN BY THE OLD MILL STREAM
  Copyright Forster Music Co.
DRINK TO ME ONLY WITH THINE EYES (BB 46) (TFB 35) (LS 53) (NASB 39) (SA 67a)
*I LOVE A LASSIE
  Copyright Music Pub. Holding Corp.
JUANITA (BB 52) (TFB 34) (LS 67) (NASB 72) (SWS 55)
*LET ME CALL YOU SWEETHEART
  Copyright Paull-Pioneer Music Corp.
LOCH LOMOND (BB 36) (TFB 102) (LS 69) (NASB 45) (SA 65a) (SWS 82)
*LONG, LONG TRAIL (BB 128) (TFB 178) —words only.
  Copyright Music Pub. Holding Corp.
LOVE'S OLD SWEET SONG (BB 45) (TFB 29) (LS 50) (NASB 115)
*MY WILD IRISH ROSE
  Copyright Music Pub. Holding Corp.
O SOLE MIO (SWS 36) (NASB 144)
*PUT ON YOUR OLD GREY BONNET
  Copyright Music Pub. Holding Corp.
*WHEN IRISH EYES ARE SMILING
  Copyright Music Pub. Holding Corp.
*THE WORLD IS WAITING FOR THE SUNRISE
  Copyright Music Pub. Holding Corp.

Hymns

ABIDE WITH ME (BB 59) (TFG 85) (NASB 157)
K. ETERNAL FATHER (Navy Hymn) (GSF 28) Copyright M. T. K.
FAITH OF OUR FATHERS (BB 140) (TFG 87) (GSF 4)
GOD BE WITH YOU TILL WE MEET AGAIN (BB 62)
GOD OF OUR FATHERS (National Hymn) (BB 132) (TFG 2) (NASB 126) (SWS 67)
LITTLE BROWN CHURCH (TFB 39) (SWS 63) (NASB 82)
A MIGHTY FORTRESS IS OUR GOD (SWS 78) (GSF 6)
NOW THE DAY IS OVER (BB 57) (TFG 86) (NASB 159) (SWS 74)
O GOD OUR HELP IN AGES PAST (BB 136) (TFB 168)
ONWARD, CHRISTIAN SOLDIERS (BB 57) (TFB 68) (NASB 153) (SWS 117) (S 137)
O WORSHIP THE KING (GSF 15)
PRAYER OF THANKSGIVING (TFG 88) (KOS 71) (NASB 58) (S 126) (SA 128) (SWS 65) (GSF 34)
K. THESE THINGS SHALL BE (GSF 2) (p. 16 of this book)

Christmas

DECK THE HALLS (BB 66) (CC 20) (TFB 78)

THE FIRST NOEL (BB 67) (CC 11) (TFB 75) (LS 95) (S 130) (STSWD 28) (Kj-octvo)

HARK, THE HERALD ANGELS SING (BB 68) (CC 23) (TFB 67)

IT CAME UPON THE MIDNIGHT CLEAR (BB 68) (CC 13)

JINGLE BELLS (BB 120) (TFB 122) (LS 88) (NASB 119) (SWS 111) (FSTSWD 14)

JOY TO THE WORLD (BB 71) (CC 31) (TFG 77) (LS 91) (S 128) (SWS 108) (FDT 33)

O COME ALL YE FAITHFUL (BB 72) (CC 9) (TFB 65) (LS 93) (S 128) (SWS 59) (FDT)

O, LITTLE TOWN OF BETHLEHEM (BB 73) (CC 13) (TFB 163) (LS 92)

SILENT NIGHT (BB 67) (CC 17) (TFB 77) (LS 90) (NASB 138) (S 127) (SWS 109) (FSTSWD 45)

Stunt Songs

HOORAY FOR THE ARMY (Tune: Yankee Doodle)
Tell me, have you heard about Harry,
   Just got back from the Army?
They say he knows how to meet defeat,
   Hip, Hip, hooray for the Army!
(Actions to fit the words!)

THE KING'S NAVEE (Tune: Old Grey Mare) (LS 29)
Oh, I don't want to march in the infantry,
   Ride in the cavalry,
Shoot the artillery,
   Oh, I don't want to fly over Germany,
I'm in the King's Navee.

I'm in the King's Navee,
I'm in the King's Navee,
(Repeat first five lines)
(Actions to suit each line)

OLD MACDONALD HAD A FARM (Fl-octvo)

THE TREE IN THE WOOD (TFG 93) (NASB 116)

CHIMNEY SONG
(Actions to fit the words)

Moderato

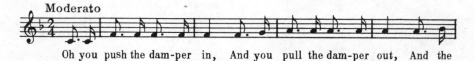

Oh you push the dam-per in, And you pull the dam-per out, And the

smoke goes up the chim-ney just the same;____ Just the same,____ just the

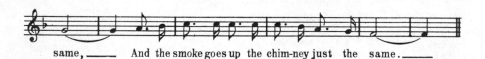

same,____ And the smoke goes up the chim-ney just the same.____

MY HAT (Tune: Carnival in Venice).

Waltz tempo

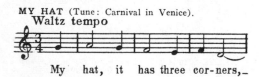

My hat, it has three cor-ners,____

____ Three cor-ners has my hat;____

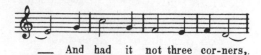

____ And had it not three cor-ners,

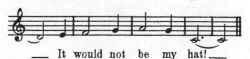

____ It would not be my hat!____

MY HAT: First time—sing straight through. Second time—tip imaginary hat instead of singing "hat." Third time—same as second, and point to elbow instead of singing "corners." Fourth time—same as third and hold up three fingers instead of singing "three."

American Folk Songs

AUNT DINAH'S QUILTING PARTY (TFB 147)

K. CIELITO LINDO (Kj-octvo) (S 45) (SA 49) (Translation copyright)

K. CHIAPANECAS (Mexican Clapping Song) (Kj-Solo-octvo) (Translation and arrangements copyright) (FDT 44)

THE ERIE CANAL (BB 41) (LS 10) (NASB 151) (S 80) (SA 64a)

GRANDMA GRUNTS (CF & GS-octvo)

HOODAH DAY (Sacramento) (SA 3)

HOME ON THE RANGE (BB 253) (LS 3) (NASB 33) (S 120) (SA 32a) (SWS 26)

IN THE EVENING BY THE MOONLIGHT (S 58) (SWS 103)

LEVEE SONG (BB 237) (TFB 54) (NASB 30)

*MAN ON THE FLYING TRAPEZE
Copyright Robbins Music Corp.

MY BONNIE (TFB 106)

POP GOES THE WEASEL (LS 33)

SHE'LL BE COMIN' ROUND THE MOUNTAIN (LS 35) (S 91)

THERE IS A TAVERN (SGN)

K. WAIT FOR THE WAGON (FDT 21)

WHOOPEE TI YI OH! (NASB 35)

Miscellaneous

AULD LANG SYNE (BB 37) (TFB 37) (LS 73) (NASB 44) (SWS 118)

BLOW THE MAN DOWN (SWS 20) (TFB 52) (NASB 69)

*PERFECT DAY (BB 128) (TFB 181)—words only. Copyright Carrie Jacobs Bond & Sons

THERE'S MUSIC IN THE AIR (BB 34) (NASB 113)